A Man's Guide to Being Catholic

A Man's Guide to Being Catholic

Mitch Finley

WIPF & STOCK · Eugene, Oregon

Wipf and Stock Publishers
199 W 8th Ave, Suite 3
Eugene, OR 97401

A Man's Guide to Being Catholic
By Finley, Mitch
Copyright©1998 by Finley, Mitch
ISBN 13: 978-1-5326-4437-5
Publication date 5/1/2018
Previously published by Liguori Publications, 1998

For Clay Barbeau

*A faithful friend is a sturdy shelter;
he who finds one finds a treasure.*
Sirach 6:14

DESPITE OUR ALL-MALE clergy, Catholicism is becoming a religion that often has too little relationship to the day-to-day activities of ordinary men. They're harried, they're worn out, they're worried about losing their jobs, they're drinking too much, they're sexually tempted, they haven't been truly excited by anything in years, but Sunday homilies too often only offer pabulum about loving one another. And love is a term drained of meaning for most men. The more deeply I read the gospels, the more I find in Jesus a tough, masculine, brook-no-guff revolutionary, a leader any man would follow if only to argue with him. But the unsettling, disquieting, complicated Jesus is usually sacrificed for a soft and tender Prince Charming who's easier to deal with.

RON HANSEN, NOVELIST,
AUTHOR OF *MARIETTE IN ECSTASY* AND *ATTICUS*

Contents

Preface: Why Choose Catholicism? xi

Introduction: Why a Book on Catholicism for Men? 1

Chapter 1: A Catholic Man's Approach to Love for God 7

Chapter 2: A Catholic Man's Approach to Faith in Christ 21

Chapter 3: A Catholic Man's Approach to the Scriptures 33

Chapter 4: A Catholic Man's Approach to the Sacraments 47

Chapter 5: A Catholic Man's Approach to Family Life 61

Chapter 6: A Catholic Man's Approach to His Parish 77

Chapter 7: A Catholic Man Follows Christ in the Church 91

Chapter 8: Catholic Men and Catholic Women 107

Afterword: A Catholic Man's Devotion to Mary 121

Notes 125

Preface
Why Choose Catholicism?

CATHOLICISM GLADLY acknowledges the goodness, truth, and beauty found in many religious and philosophical traditions. "The Catholic Church rejects nothing of what is true and holy in these religions," declared the Second Vatican Council in 1965.[1]

In this broad-minded, tolerant era, therefore, I owe it to the reader to explain why I prefer Catholicism. I admire the explanation given by G. K. Chesterton, a great early-twentieth-century English writer and Catholic convert. In his book *The Well and the Shallows* Chesterton wrote:

> I could not abandon the faith, without falling back on something more shallow than the faith. I could not cease to be a Catholic except by becoming something more narrow than a Catholic.[2]

In my book *The Seeker's Guide to Being Catholic* I wrote that "'narrow-minded Catholic' is an oxymoron," and it's true.[3] I prefer Catholicism because it is *catholic,* with a lowercase *c,* which means "universal" and "all-inclusive." Catholicism at its best is the only religion that is open to whatever is good, true, and beautiful in all other religions, philosophies, and perspectives and more. Look closely at other religions, sects, traditions, perspectives, and philosophies, and sooner or later you will find that each one shuts the door on something that Catholicism welcomes. At the same time, if you find something that Catholicism rejects or doesn't care for, you will find that it is something incomplete or something less than good, true, or beautiful.

Perhaps the best example from our era of someone with a truly Catholic perspective is Thomas Merton. The famous Trappist monk and author appreciated deeply all the goodness, truth, and beauty he found in Judaism, Islam, Sufism, and Buddhism, as well as in Protestant forms of Christianity. He learned from the works of believers, to be sure, but he also learned from intellectuals and artists who were agnostics, atheists, and skeptics. Yet all the while he remained a Catholic and saw no conflict between his Catholic faith and, for example, the incorporation of Zen meditation into his own spirituality.

The Catholic Church is both a human institution and a divine mystery, an imperfect means to an eternal end, in this world and the next, and as such it has its faults and failings. Catholics and their institutions have blind spots and a shadow side, as do all things in time and space. All the same, to make Chesterton's perspective my own, I prefer Catholicism because to choose something other than Catholicism I would need to choose something that, sooner or later, would prove to be narrower and shallower than Catholicism.

A Man's Guide to Being Catholic

Introduction

Why a Book on Catholicism for Men?

WE LIVE in a feminist era, both in the world and in the Church. There is no way this book could begin without acknowledging that fact. The self-understanding of women, men's understanding of women, and women's understanding of men are basic to many contemporary social and personal issues. It would seem, therefore, than any book for men, or about men, must respond to feminism. This may be inevitable and, indeed, desirable. All the same, this book will focus on a discussion of issues of primary concern to men, responding to feminist concerns along the way. More specifically, the focus is on Catholic men and how they might approach Catholicism as a living faith, a spirituality, and a way of life precisely *as men*.

Clearly, men and women are similar in more ways than they are different. Still, the differences are significant, and we ignore them at our own peril. Two best-selling books, *You Just Don't Understand Me* by Deborah Tannen (Ballantine Books, 1991) and *Men Are from Mars, Women Are from Venus* by John

Gray (HarperCollins, 1992), illustrate the point. The popularity of these books reflects the widespread conviction that we need to pay attention to ways in which men and women are unique. This book reflects informally and in a nonsystematic way on male uniqueness in an explicitly Roman Catholic context.

The approach of this book is Christological. Jesus of Nazareth was a man, and Christian men should look to him as their model. Catholic women may—indeed, must—do the same, but how they do that is not this book's concern. Is it significant that Jesus of Nazareth was a man and not a woman? Let scholars of both sexes wrestle with this question, and good luck to them all. Jesus of Nazareth was a man, the gospels take his maleness for granted, and this book looks to the Jesus of the gospels for insights into a man's approach to being a Catholic and a Catholic approach to being a man.

The maleness of Jesus is no reason for men to boast or women to be offended. It is simply an objective historical fact, and there is no reason to pretend otherwise. But Jesus' maleness is not irrelevant. We acknowledge it and pay close attention to see if men can learn something from it. Both men and women need to develop psychologically healthy and theologically sound ways to relate to this historical fact. This book is one male author's contribution to that project. Female authors are, obviously, free to do something similar from female perspectives.

Feminist authors sometimes suggest that the risen Christ, because of his risen condition, is beyond gender. It is true that in the gospels' post-Resurrection accounts the disciples sometimes fail to recognize the risen Christ. But the gospels supply no evidence to support the notion that he has become androgynous.

Although Jesus will be our primary resource and model for understanding how men may approach Catholicism, we will look to other scriptural figures who may help us with our search for a better understanding of a male approach to being Catholic. Joseph, the husband of Mary and, for all practical purposes, Jesus' father, will have his moment in the sun. David, boy shepherd and slayer of Goliath, military hero and king of Israel, will have his moment, too.

Virtually all the books not written from a fundamentalist Christian perspective about what it means to be a man today have been based on various psychological and/or psycho-theological perspectives. More than a few of these take as their starting point the work of the great twentieth-century psychologist Carl G. Jung. The author has read these books and is aware of the *anima* and *animus* theory of the male and female psyches.

Even the books written about masculine spirituality rely heavily on psychology from humanistic and Jungian perspectives.[1] Some of the most popular discussions of maleness and masculinity rely on psychological analyses of biblical stories and mythical folktales. While insights from studies such as these have their place, this book is more explicitly theological in a popular, sometimes even devotional, vein. The point is not that theology can ignore the insights of the human sciences. Rather, at some point even a popular theology needs to clear its throat, then stand up and speak for itself, say something in its own language, on its own terms and on its own authority.

While other books offer food for the intellect—an important contribution, to be sure—this book proposes to offer food for the male Catholic heart as well as the mind: nourishment for the male Catholic soul. Jesus the man who was God's own Son is our inspiration, guide, and goal. For Catholic men seek not just to follow Jesus but to become *like* Jesus and to mirror Jesus, each in his own unique fashion.

We will focus, in great part, on the images, words, and actions of Jesus in the gospels. We will avoid the suggestion of a rosy or gruesome Jesus found in pious art—no more bearded lady!—the images of a sentimental or folksy Jesus found in popular religious music, and the emasculated images of Jesus found in movies made about him. The Jesus of the gospels is the only reliable model we have, and he was the biggest surprise and the greatest blessing the earth has ever known.

In the Gospel of Mark, for example, as Patrick Arnold, S.J., remarks, "Jesus *roars* out of the desert and all hell breaks loose; throughout the rest of the work, Jesus is a man of electric power and masculine energy, a figure of great personal magnetism whom any man would be excited to follow."[2]

The Jesus of the gospels will be our guide, inspiration, and goal, but we will view Jesus from different angles and unique perspectives. We must acknowledge, of course, that each of the four gospels presents a special portrait of Jesus, a unique understanding of who and what Jesus was and is. So we will discover unique insights from the gospels along the way. At the same time, we will reflect on contemporary human experience.

Understandably, much of the "action" in Catholic circles today takes its identity or inspiration from feminist issues. But faced with claims that women are oppressed by patriarchalism and male delusions of superiority, men sometimes conclude that they have but two options. They can oppose or acquiesce to women's demands for change. They can reject or accept inclusive liturgical language with regard to both people and God. They can oppose or support calls for the ordination of women. And so forth.

The trouble is, this leaves men standing around chanting either "Us, too" or "Like hell we will," with no prior healthy self-understanding. Both reactions are merely impulsive, indicating that these men have no clear male Catholic self-image except in the context of a response to Catholic feminists. But who we are as men (and women) is only partially determined by our relationships with the other sex. A man needs a healthy, balanced understanding of himself *as male* in order to relate well to women. A woman needs a balanced, healthy *female* self-understanding in order to relate well to men. Granted, "male and female he created them" (Genesis 1:27), and *together* woman and man reflect the image of God, but neither man nor woman should allow the other to absorb his or her unique identity.

This book offers some admittedly tentative suggestions about how Catholic *men* reflect the image of God. About how, in today's world, a man can be a Catholic, live a Catholic life and spirituality, be happier with himself, and be a more complete person for that fact.

One book cannot hope to present a definitive answer, but it can make a beginning.

Chapter 1
A Catholic Man's Approach to Love for God

IN THE GOSPELS, Jesus leaves no doubt about his priorities:

> One of the scribes came near and heard them disputing with one another, and seeing that [Jesus] answered them well, he asked him, "Which commandment is the first of all?" Jesus answered, "The first is, 'Hear, O Israel: the Lord our God, the Lord is one; you shall love the Lord your God with all your heart, and with all your soul, and with all your mind, and with all your strength.' The second is this, 'You shall love your neighbor as yourself.' There is no other commandment greater than these" (Mark 12:28–31).

Catholic men know these words of Jesus well, having heard them read countless times in the context of the Eucharist and through their own reading of the gospels. We know that Jesus' great commandment is to love God with one's whole being and "your neighbor as yourself." For men, to love one's neighbor as oneself is not a difficult idea. It is simple to translate "neighbor" as spouse, children, co-workers, "the poor," and so forth. The notion of loving God, however, is another matter. It seems to be such an abstraction. Love God? Yet Jesus' instruction to love God is so basic to a complete Christian life that no man can afford to miss his point.

The man Jesus directs his disciples—and most of his disciples were men—to love God directly. This can only mean that a man must make time to be with God, to express his love for God, and to experience and learn of God's love for him. Love of neighbor is basic to a Christian life, to be sure, and opportunities to express it are not scarce. All the same, a balanced life requires time for prayerful attention to God alone.

"Just as we must eat and think and play, or else we wither and die," wrote Father Edward Collins Vacek, S.J., "and just as we must develop good relations with other human beings if we are to develop as persons, so also we cannot hope to become fully human unless we love God.…We have a native desire for God, and our hearts will shrivel up unless they beat for God. Hence, in order to become fully who we are, we must be growing in love for God."[1]

Jesus, fully a male human being as well as fully divine, gives us his own personal example of love for God. Many times in the gospels he makes time to be alone with his Father: "And after he had dismissed the crowds, he went up the mountain by himself to pray" (Matthew 14:23); "After saying farewell to them, he went up on the mountain to pray" (Mark 6:46); "But he would withdraw to deserted places and pray" (Luke 5:16); "Now during those days he went out to the mountain to pray; and he spent the night in prayer to God" (Luke 6:12). The man Jesus clearly has a deep love for his Father, a deep love for

God, and he invites men and women to follow his example. But in our culture men are more inclined than women to overlook that example. This would be a mistake, because if Jesus is our model of authentic manhood, then authentic manhood requires growth in prayerfulness. Real men, like Jesus of the gospels, love God and spend time loving God directly in prayer.

A *bon mot* from internationally popular speaker and author Clayton C. Barbeau applies: "Where you put your time you put your life, and where you put your life you put your love."[2]

This idea bears repeating: there is nothing unmasculine about spending time with God in prayer. On the contrary, if the man Jesus makes this a priority, the same must be true for men who follow Jesus today.

Failure to cultivate a life of prayer is neglect of one's inner life and spirituality and results in alienation from one's true self and from one's feelings. Women sometimes accuse men of being insensitive, lacking warmth, and being out of touch with their feelings. Unfortunately, our culture often leaves men feeling uncomfortable with the idea of being religious, much less prayerful. In our culture, religion is for women and children, the elderly, and men who need a "crutch" in order to cope. The assumption, of course, is that such people "need" religion because they are weak. Pure and simple, this form of cultural prejudice is an insult to all religious persons.

It is also an insult to Catholicism, which is anything but a crutch for the weak. It takes a special kind of inner strength and courage for a man to take religion seriously, particularly in our culture. The dominant popular culture smiles indulgently at religion in general and Catholicism in particular. In many circles populated by sophisticated, well-educated people, it is fashionable to mock the Catholic Church as a haven for the weak, the guilt-ridden, the simpleminded, the enchained. The youth subculture also scorns religion. You're not about to see MTV encouraging church attendance.

Contrast this with cultures that are completely spiritual. Thomas Merton, the great Trappist monk, author, and spiritual master, was deeply impressed in Bangkok, Thailand, by an entire culture rooted in religion and spirituality. There he saw everyone, men and women, take for granted the spiritual nature of all things, and he saw prayer practiced as a natural part of everyday life.[3]

Catholicism is a way of life—a culture—not a religious formality reserved for Sundays and holidays. Love of God, love of neighbor, and awareness of God's presence in the ordinary form the basis for this way of life.

In practical terms, this means that Catholic men need to make time to love God through personal prayer, for at least a few minutes each day. The form prayer takes will vary from man to man. If any guideline is important to a man's spirituality today it is this one: Pray in ways that work for you.

The habit of prayer, however, is a response to an experience men frequently do not have in our culture. That experience is the feeling or perception that "God loves me." It is relatively unusual for men to know from personal experience, not just intellectually, that God loves them with an overwhelming, passionate, unconditional love. Many men are mystified when they hear someone talk about this love because they have never experienced it for themselves. What are such men to do? Until they experience God's love personally, men are unlikely to know what it means to make their Catholic faith the foundation of their daily lives.

One way men can come to experience God's love is by participating in a group retreat. A men's retreat can sometimes have a profound impact on men, but the risk is that in such situations a man's response, even unconsciously, will be to group expectations rather than to a personal experience of God's unconditional love. Once the tight-knit social context and the social pressure of the group retreat is gone, a man can all too easily revert to old habits devoid of an orientation to the love of God. As a result, the most effective and long-lasting, as well as simplest, way to experience God's love directly is through prayerful solitude.

It takes courage, fortitude, and a readiness to risk for a man to enter into a few days of prayerful solitude and silence. Some men may experience such deep anxiety at the very thought of it that they would be wise to consult a spiritual director before attempting such an exercise, even if it's only for a weekend. Conditioned to a culture that bombards our senses with technology and pummels them with commercials, a man can experience quite a shock in finding himself alone, in a very quiet place, with nothing except a Bible, a book or two, and perhaps a rosary. Our culture conditions the average man to be constantly on the go, active, assertive, working, making things happen. It takes nerve, it takes guts to freely give oneself to even a few days away from all that. It takes courage to face oneself and God with no way to escape. Silence and solitude are not for the weak of heart.

Yet it is in prayerful solitude and silence that a man can "wait for the LORD" (Psalm 37:34). It is in prayerful solitude that a man can face himself directly. Paradoxically, when that happens, he will find himself face-to-face with the God who loves him with an endless love. For if you find yourself, you will find God; and if you find God, you will find yourself. The two discoveries go hand in hand.

With prayerful patience, a man in solitude will have a personal experience of God's overwhelming love for him. Soon, he will find it easy to respond to that love, loving God in return. Even the most momentary feeling of being loved by God will lead to a feeling of gratitude and joy. To know God's infinite love is to begin a lifelong process of wanting to love God, in return, for his own sake.

The reason a man requires silence and solitude in order to discover his true self and experience God's love is that so much of the world we live in is permeated by what Thomas Merton called "unreality." Merton wrote, "There is no greater disaster in the spiritual life than to be immersed in unreality, for life is maintained and nourished in us by our vital relation with realities outside and above us. When our life feeds on unreality, it must starve. It must die."[4] We live in our culture like a fish swims in water, and much of what we respond to—and many of our expectations, wants, desires, and hopes—is rooted in unreality. The entertainment industry, for example, thrives on unreality. Movies, television sitcoms, and the advertising industry driving these entertainments present unreal images of people, human relationships, and the world. We may think that years and decades of exposure to these images have no effect on us—that we are above all that. Still, they have their impact on our heart, mind, and soul.

Take sex, for example. The entertainment and advertising industries constantly fill the male mind and imagination with unreal images of "ideal" human bodies, male and female. We tend to compare ourselves and the women we know unfavorably with these "ideals," and these comparisons have a negative impact on our marriages or possible future marriages, not to mention our relationships with women in general. Additionally, movies and television programs portray sexual encounters in unreal ways, ways no real human couple ever experiences. All the same, these unreal Hollywood images shape our imaginations, and we tend to compare our own sexual experiences unfavorably with these images.

Another example of the unreality that permeates our culture—an unreality to which men, in particular, are susceptible—is the cultural pressure to equate love with limitless economic security. In our culture, there is no such thing as "enough," especially when it comes to financial resources. In our culture, Mammon is God and the *Wall Street Journal* is its prophet. From this unreal perspective, the most loving action a "family man" can take is to generate as much money as possible as fast as possible. If a man "loves" his wife and children, he must show his love by working, working, working, staying away from his family much of the time in order to make more money. "Love" means providing as much "economic security" as possible, as affluent a lifestyle as possible, and as many things as possible.

Down deep, this outlook is rooted in unreality. What is real is the gift of self, not the dumping of money on one's family. Of course, a family needs and has a right to a certain minimum of economic security. We all need food, clothing, and a roof over our heads. We need proper medical care. But in general we need much less money, and far less affluence, than our culture would have us believe. There comes a point when a man's family needs him, present and accounted for, far more than they need more money. To spend a lifetime scratching for a higher level of affluence is to spend a lifetime grasping at unreality.

Unreality is glitzy, but its promises are false. Unless we take steps to distance ourselves from it and expose ourselves more to reality, the result can be disastrous. Steeped in unreality, we become dissatisfied with reality. "When our life feeds on unreality, it must starve."

A real life must feed on the ultimate reality: our God who loves us unconditionally and constantly draws us to life and to all that is good, true, beautiful, and real. To make time, each day, to love God in prayer is to expose ourselves to this reality. To take a few minutes each day for prayerful reading of the Scriptures, or praying of the rosary, or reading of some prayerful meditations is to adopt a Catholic countercultural stance, is to swim upstream, is to position yourself for choices that will lead to risky moves and a life worth living. Even so small a choice as this roots a man in his Catholic faith in life-changing ways.

Whether in solitude or as a daily discipline—and sometimes, "discipline" is exactly the right word, because often it takes determination, a definite act of "willpower"—one of the most beneficial forms of prayer for a man is called *lectio divina*. The Latin words mean "holy reading," but the Latin term is used most commonly. There is nothing esoteric or difficult about *lectio divina*. It is an ancient but simple approach to praying with Scripture, one ideally suited to balancing a man's busy, active life with a few minutes of open, receptive prayer.

Nothing could be simpler. Step one: Sit down, quiet down, and take a deep breath to calm yourself. Step two: Open your Bible. Step three: Begin reading, slowly, one of the psalms, a passage from one of the gospels, or whatever appeals to you. Step four: When a particular phrase or word grabs your attention and touches your heart, stop reading, close your eyes, and allow the word or phrase to repeat itself, over and over, in your heart. Step five: When that word or phrase has emptied itself, continue reading, repeating the process.

This, in a nutshell, is *lectio divina*. It can last for as long as you want it to, and anyone can find ten or fifteen minutes during even a busy day for *lectio divina*.

When practiced regularly, *lectio divina*, as any form of prayer, increases a man's sensitivity to God's presence in every dimension of his life. Giving time to prayer a few minutes each day results in greater patience with one's family, greater resilience in coping with life's pressures, and an increased ability to make good choices about the use of time, money, and other resources. In other words, prayer nourishes faith, one's loving intimacy with God—which means your life will "come together" in beneficial, sometimes unexpected ways.

Loving God regularly in prayer is rooted in the experience of being loved by God. The Hebrew Scriptures, or Old Testament, contains 173 references to God's "steadfast love" (NRSV), this absolutely reliable love of God for his people. For example, "Be mindful of your mercy, O Lord, / and of your steadfast love, / for they have been from of old. / Do not remember the sins of my youth or my transgressions; / according to your steadfast love remember me, / for your goodness' sake, O Lord!" sings the psalmist (25:6–7).

A man's experience of God's love, and his love for God in return, takes on a certain poignant importance in our culture because men are so often motivated in their actions and lifestyle choices by what can only be described as anxious fear. Although the cultural ideal of manhood is a blend of football-field stamina (in the workplace) and gruff kindness (at home), men are frequently motivated deep inside by anxious fear of what the future may bring in both arenas.

In the workplace, the future may bring outright unemployment, lack of long-term job stability, or insufficient income to maintain an increasing level of affluence. At home, men are anxious and fearful about measuring up to social and domestic expectations. Our culture is uncertain about the male identity and ambivalent about male roles in the home. Feminism places still other pressures on men, mostly pushing them to be more domestic and nurturing, to fill roles for which they had few, if any, role models as they were growing up.

Frequently, men are also anxious and fearful about their children. What is a "good" father supposed to do today? Men are unsure how to help kids grow into healthy, mature adults in a society that places kids at risk with regard to everything from alcohol and nicotine to drugs and irresponsible, sometimes life-threatening sexual behaviors.

The ultimate source of anxious fear is, of course, death. A man can trace most of his anxiety to a fear of death. Say a man is fearful about losing his job. The most immediate source of this fear is his concern that he be able to contribute to his family's income so the bills can be paid, food can be put on the table, and a home be maintained for his family to live in. Even when a man's spouse works, too, which is almost always the case today, many families find it nearly impossible to survive on one income alone. So a man fears losing his job because he fears homelessness and hunger. But behind these fears is the greater terror that homelessness and hunger could lead to worse—ultimately, to death. The dark shadow of death, of nonbeing, powers the fear that fills a man's heart when he worries about unemployment.

Still, any life is filled with dangers that *might* happen. Insurance companies make money by capitalizing on people's worries about what might happen. Buying a life-insurance policy may be a perfectly practical step, but the man of faith will realize that financial forms of security are limited. To buy a life-insurance policy out of simple levelheaded prudence is one thing; to do so out of fear is another. When push comes to shove, only the love of God can satisfy a man's longing for a reliable source of security. In the end, only the love of God will free a man from the fear that motivates the choices he makes and the goals he sets for himself.

A man's love for God is his ultimate source of security in an uncertain world, but it is the kind of security that comes from faith, not the kind of security that comes from insurance policies. A man who follows Jesus' example and gives his heart to God, who carves out a few minutes each day for prayer, who knows and appreciates the value of prayerful solitude, is a man who will have a deeply rooted sense of self-assurance in a world filled with risks and uncertainty—a man who will be able to live with confidence.

"Do not worry about anything," Saint Paul advises in the Letter to the Philippians, "but in everything by prayer and supplication with thanksgiving let your requests be made known to God. And the peace of God, which surpasses all understanding, will guard your hearts and your minds in Christ Jesus" (4:6–7). Paul is not merely hawking pious platitudes here. When he declares that we should not worry about anything, he means that we should not worry about *anything*. Paul does not say that we should stop thinking about the things we need to think about, or stop being concerned with what we need to be concerned with. He does mean that we should not *worry* about these things. Be concerned, yes. Cope, yes. Deal with reality, yes. Do all you can do, but while you do it, and when you have done it, then give it to God in prayer. Then you will have "the peace of God, which surpasses all understanding."

More often than not, this is where the rubber hits the road for men, and this is where a Catholic man can strengthen his faith by looking to the Jesus of the gospels. In Matthew's Gospel, particularly, Jesus places great emphasis on the need not to worry and the need to trust completely in the love of God: "Therefore, I tell you, do not worry…" (6:25); "And why do you worry…?" (6:28); "Therefore do not worry…" (6:31); "So do not worry about tomorrow…" (6:34); "…do not worry…" (10:19).

We know that Jesus is not mouthing pious platitudes either,

because the gospels tell us that even in his most fearful moments, in the Garden of Gethsemane, he abandons himself to his Father's love. Notice, Jesus does not become Mister Calm, Cool, and Collected. He is terribly upset. Matthew's Gospel describes Jesus in Gethsemane as "deeply grieved" (26:36). Mark's Gospel says that Jesus is "distressed and agitated" (14:33), and Jesus tells his disciples that he is "deeply grieved, even to death" (14:34). In a more colloquial translation of this verse, Jesus says, "I am so sad that I feel as if I am dying" (CEV). The Gospel of Luke is even more dramatic: "In his anguish he prayed more earnestly, and his sweat became like great drops of blood falling down on the ground" (22:44).

Is Jesus a man in touch with his feelings? He does not pretend that he is not afraid. He accepts his fear and sadness, and in Mark, the earliest gospel, he openly admits how he feels to his disciples. But Jesus' feelings do not call the shots. Jesus doesn't wallow in his feelings, and he doesn't allow them to control his behavior. Yes, he is anxious and afraid, but he is a "stand-up guy," a man who faces even death with trust in his Father's love. This Jesus is a man's man when it comes to the issue of anxious fear.

Here is the tough, genuinely masculine response to anxious fear that Jesus models for men today, a response rooted not in fear but in love. Anxiety and fear exist, but love is stronger. Even in the midst of sadness, fear, and anxiety, Jesus acts on the conviction that nothing is more certain than his Father's love.

A Catholic man models himself on the Jesus of the gospels and develops the will to trust in God's steadfast loving-kindness by living his daily life in loving intimacy with God, loving God and being open to God's love for him. A Catholic man is a man of prayer according to the model of the man Jesus, whose masculinity is beyond question, and so his love for God is deep, resilient, and prepared to take risks based on loving intimacy with God. In this way, a Catholic man attains his own unique identity and finds a firm footing in a world filled with uncertainty.

Chapter 2

A Catholic Man's Approach to Faith in Christ

THE CONCEPT of Christian faith is a peculiar one because it is so often misconstrued. People toss around the term *Christian faith* like a beanbag, everyone assuming that everyone agrees on its meaning. The exact contrary is the case, of course. What many people mean by Christian faith is different from the Catholic meaning of the term. Most modern, with-it folks think that Christian faith is, for all practical purposes, "blind faith." They think that to have Christian faith is to believe in something unreasonable. Or they think that Christian faith means to accept a moral or ethical code simply because "the Bible" or "the Church" says so, once again, with no basis in reason or even common sense.

This typical understanding of Christian faith is laughable. When Catholicism says "faith," it means several things, but the most basic meaning of faith, from a Catholic perspective, is mystical and might be stated briefly in this manner: *Christian faith is a personal relationship with the risen Christ, and with his people, the Church, that results in a freedom and a security that transcend but do not do away with everyday insecurity.* As we proceed with our discussion, each part of this Catholic understanding of faith will become clearer.

Faith is first of all, and last of all, a personal relationship with the risen Christ and with his people, the Church. For Catholic men in particular, this means cultivating an ongoing communion with the risen Christ, learning from the Jesus of the gospels, and participating in the life of the wider Church, and the world, where he is present and active.

Here we must highlight an important distinction between faith and the institutions that are supposed to nourish faith. Abraham Joshua Heschel (1907–1972) was a Jewish philosopher and commentator on the place of religion in modern society. What he says of religion in general is true of Catholicism:

> When faith is completely replaced by creed, worship by discipline, love by habit; when the crisis of today is ignored because of the splendor of the past; when faith becomes an heirloom rather than a living fountain; when religion speaks only in the name of authority rather than with the voice of compassion, its message becomes meaningless.[1]

When we mistake the institutions and traditions of Catholicism for faith, then faith is lost. It becomes a "nostalgia trip" or a way to escape responsibility for one's own life. Catholic institutions and traditions exist to support and nourish faith, not to replace it. The official teachings of the Church are there to shape and guide personal conscience, not replace it. As a religion, Catholicism exists to support, guide, and facilitate our relationships with the risen Christ, with one another, and with the earth, our home. But religion will make sense only as long as a man keeps his eyes on the Jesus of the gospels and his heart attuned to the risen Christ alive in his own being and active in the Church and in the world.

In other words, a man's faith and his participation in the life of the Church depend most basically on his relationship with the risen Christ. The two are interdependent, of course, but the foundation is a man's ongoing intimacy with Christ. As we saw in chapter 1, a man remains in communion with the risen Christ through daily prayer and devotion.

For further insights into the nature of a Catholic man's faith in Christ, we turn to the Gospel of Mark. Scholarly consensus identifies this gospel, written about the year A.D. 70, as the oldest of the four and the one source both Matthew and Luke share in common. In Mark we find the earliest account of who Jesus was, in the light of the Resurrection, for the early Christian community. Mark's Jesus is still rough around the edges, less polished, one step closer to the gritty Jesus who walked the dusty roads of Palestine than the Jesus we find in the other three gospels.[2]

The first person to appear in Mark's Gospel is not Jesus but John the Baptizer, and Mark's portrait of him is both concise and stark:

> John the baptizer appeared in the wilderness, proclaiming a baptism of repentance for the forgiveness of sins. And people from the whole Judean countryside and all the people of Jerusalem were going out to him, and were baptized by him in the river Jordan, confessing their sins. Now John was clothed with camel's hair, with a leather belt around his waist, and he ate locusts and wild honey. He proclaimed, "The one who is more powerful than I is coming after me; I am not worthy to stoop down and untie the

thong of his sandals. I have baptized you with water; but he will baptize you with the Holy Spirit" (1:4–8).

Mark first identifies Jesus by contrasting him with John, whom he calmly describes as a wild man. Indeed, John is the last of the Old Testament prophets: all that business about wearing garments of camel's hair, with a leather belt, and eating locusts and wild honey strikes the modern ear as a shocking lifestyle. John is definitely a rough-and-tumble character. But notice: John himself insists that he is a wimp compared with Jesus. After all that rough living out in the desert, John is no weakling, but he openly declares that Jesus is stronger, "more powerful."

John also insists that compared with Jesus, he is less than a slave. Part of a slave's or servant's job description would be to untie the master's sandals in order to wash his feet, but John says that when it comes to Jesus, he does not have even the status of a slave. John might as well have said, "Compared to Jesus, I'm lower than dirt."

Is the Jesus of Mark's Gospel a "bearded lady," a weakling, a spineless patsy? Not a chance. If Mark's Jesus can make even an extraordinarily powerful man such as John the Baptizer step aside, then he must be strong, assertive, and masculine, able to take care of himself, and possessed of incredible dignity and power.

At the same time, Mark's Jesus is not only deeply spiritual but also committed to a religious mission. The tough, roughly clad, locust-chewing John recognizes this. Whereas John merely pours water over people, or dunks them in the muddy river as a sign of repentance, Jesus will immerse people in the Holy Spirit. Mark's first readers would have been most impressed by this distinction because when they heard "Holy Spirit," they would have known that John was talking about God, not some pious devotional subtlety. Jesus would bathe people in the very Spirit of God, an experience almost beyond comprehension but a sure sign of spiritual healing and liberation in both this world and the next.

In the Gospel of Mark, then, Jesus' spiritual nature and religious mission are basic to his masculinity. And when we follow Jesus as our model, we see that to be a man requires attention to one's spirituality and faith. Rather than being a sign of weakness or inadequacy, living a life rooted in God is a sign of strength, power, and liberation.

Mark's narrative continues:

> In those days Jesus came from Nazareth of Galilee and was baptized by John in the Jordan. And just as he was coming up out of the water, he saw the heavens torn apart and the Spirit descending like a dove on him. And a voice came from heaven, "You are my Son, the Beloved; with you I am well pleased."
>
> And the Spirit immediately drove him out into the wilderness. He was in the wilderness forty days, tempted by Satan; and he was with the wild beasts; and the angels waited on him (1:9–13).

Mark's Jesus is a model of manhood that has nothing to do with macho swagger. When Jesus submits himself to John's baptism, although he is more powerful, he does not insist that John acknowledge his superiority. He does not saunter up to John and say, "See here, fool, I'm the one doing the baptizing now, so *I* will baptize *you*." The gospel tells us that Jesus leaves his hometown of Nazareth, arrives at the Jordan River, quietly steps into the stream, and accepts baptism by John. Jesus certainly does not grovel, but neither does he insist that John give way to him. The more powerful willingly submits to ritual initiation by the less powerful. The one with the greater status and dignity calmly accepts baptism by an inferior. The one who is without sin participates in a ritual of repentance as if he actually needs it.

Jesus reveals his power, strength, and courage not by flaunting them but by identifying himself with the mass of humanity. Jesus joins the human race, descending into the water and undergoing a baptism ritual, thus foreshadowing the baptism required by those who would follow him. Jesus might as well have said, preposterous as it sounds, "We are all in this together, and I am with you in everything, from beginning to end." Preposterous, but true. The man Jesus shows men by his own example that it is important to participate in the rites and rituals of the community.

In our own time, many "with it" people may snicker at the idea of "going to church." Our culture idealizes macho images of men in western garb who ride horses and squat around a campfire and drink beer; men who shoot pool, whop one another on the back, and drink beer; men who climb into race cars, roar around a track, and drink beer; men who take up high-powered rifles, fire them at various forms of wildlife, and drink beer; three-hundred-pound men who don football pads, crash into one another, and drink beer.

The only alternative, in Western cultures, is of more recent vintage. The fabulously wealthy computer geek also demands respect, so men may with honor strive to fashion themselves after this model as well. In both cases, however—the traditional macho-man model and the more recent computer-geek model—the ideal is for a man to throw his weight around, either physically or economically. If a man can't be *on* a football team, then he should *own* a football team.

These models dominate the media, especially mass-market advertising, but advertisers are not stupid. Now and then, ad agencies give a nod to a nurturing model of manhood. You see a strong male portrayed holding an infant, for example, or men interacting with family members—"softer," more domestic portraits. Such images amount to little more than tokenism, and none of these models of what it means to be a male include spirituality or participation in the rituals and rites of a religious tradition. Not a one.

The Gospel of Mark uses powerful images to show that Jesus' model of manhood has strong ties not just to rites and rituals but to mystical experience also. Coming up out of the river after receiving John's baptism, the mud between his toes, Jesus sees "the heavens torn apart and the Spirit descending like a dove on him. And a voice came from heaven, 'You are my Son, the Beloved; with you I am well pleased.'"

Notice, the heavens are "torn apart"; they don't open up into a Helen Steiner Rice greeting-card illustration, the rays of the sun beaming down on a pastoral landscape. For Mark's Gospel to say that Jesus sees the heavens "torn apart" is yet another indication that for the man Jesus this is a wild experience, not a tame one—an adventure, not a vacation.

How does the Spirit act next? In an astonishing fashion: "And the Spirit immediately drove him out into the wilderness. He was in the wilderness forty days, tempted by Satan; and he was with the wild beasts; and the angels waited on him." The Spirit does not "gently lead" Jesus into the wilderness. The Spirit does not "encourage" Jesus to go out into the wilderness. The Spirit does not "suggest" that Jesus go into the wilderness. The Spirit forcefully pushes Jesus. The Greek word translated "drove" is *ekballei,* and it means "to drive out or throw out forcibly." Matthew's Gospel uses this word when it says that Jesus "casts out" a demon (9:34), and when it says that Jesus "drove out" the moneychangers from the temple (21:12).

For the man Jesus to accept his mission as Son of God, he must immediately accept being pushed around by the Spirit, out into a desert wilderness where he has nothing but "wild beasts" for company and temptations from Satan to occupy his mind and heart. Does this kind of thing happen to Mary, in Luke's Gospel, when she accepts her mission to become the mother of God's Son? No. When Mary affirms the angel's message, the next event is a visit with her cousin, Elizabeth, and glad hosannas (see Luke 1:38–56). It's different for Jesus. He gets forty days with wild beasts in the wilderness and temptations from Satan.

Mark's Gospel concludes this account, of course, with the announcement that "angels waited on him"—which is good to know. Notice, however, that the business about angels comes at the end, *after* the wild beasts and the temptations from Satan. The message may be that only after Jesus faces up to the painful realities does he get some relief. Certainly this will prove to be the case when it comes to his death and Resurrection.

Regardless, we may take this account of the Spirit's pushing Jesus out into the Judaean wilderness as a metaphor for his passage into full manhood and final acceptance of his divine mission. As a fully human man, Jesus had also to accept and affirm his identity as Son of God and Messiah. In this sense, Jesus stands as a model for all men who must choose between identifying as adopted sons of God and brothers of Jesus, and acceding to the dominant culture's trivialization of maleness. This is a choice that all men must make.

Having made his choice, Jesus embarks on his mission and calls his first disciples. According to Mark's Gospel:

As Jesus passed along the Sea of Galilee, he saw Simon and his brother Andrew casting a net into the sea—for they were fishermen. And Jesus said to them, "Follow me and I will make you fish for people." And immediately they left their nets and followed him. As he went a little farther, he saw James son of Zebedee and his brother John, who were in their boat mending the nets. Immediately he called them; and they left their father Zebedee in the boat with the hired men, and followed him (1:16–20).

The point is not that Jesus asks his disciples never to work for a living after they choose to follow him. Rather, discipleship requires the acceptance of right priorities, and security is not the top priority, particularly economic security. The top priority is to follow Jesus in all things and to draw others to the kingdom of God by the ways we live.

Notice, again, that all the characters in this account are male. These are men who leave their families and their livelihoods behind and follow Jesus. Here is a clear statement that Jesus sometimes asks men to make real sacrifices in order to be his disciples.

Don't think that this event was a ho-hummer. We need to read between the lines to get the full picture. The calling of Simon and Andrew, and James and John had to have been a powerful, upsetting event for all concerned. Zebedee, the father of James and John, must have had a fit as his two sons wandered off after this stranger, this character neither he nor his sons had ever seen before.

Something about Jesus, something about the power of his personality was enough to get these four men to drop everything and tag along after him for parts unknown.

They went to Capernaum; and when the sabbath came, he entered the synagogue and taught. They were astounded at his teaching, for he taught them as one having authority, and not as the scribes (Mark 1:21–22).

Off go the four men after Jesus, around the Sea of Galilee, to Capernaum, traveling for we don't know how many days. But on the sabbath Jesus goes into the synagogue and begins to teach. As impressed as they had been with Jesus in the first place, the four men are knocked out by his teaching; "astounded," Mark says. For Jesus teaches "as one having authority." Jesus is a man who commands attention by his presence, and when he speaks in the synagogue they can't help paying attention. Here is someone worth listening to; here is someone who knows what he is talking about.

Powerful speakers down through history have been able to control whole nations, for good or for ill. In the 1930s and 1940s, Adolf Hitler, a madman, led an entire nation into unspeakably evil acts by the sheer power of his personality and his ability as a speaker. In England, Winston Churchill did the same and rallied his nation to defend itself with great courage against overwhelming odds.

We should not be surprised that Jesus would amaze his listeners by the power of his speaking. Instead, we should listen ourselves. We should listen as men to the words of the greatest man and the most mysterious, most authoritative speaker who ever lived. Jesus spoke and men listened, overcome by the power of his words.

At this point in the gospel, Jesus works his first miracle of healing. Mark's description of this event is graphic, and you can easily see how onlookers would be struck dumb by what they witnessed:

Just then there was in their synagogue a man with an unclean spirit, and he cried out, "What have you to do with us, Jesus of Nazareth? Have you come to destroy us? I know who you are, the Holy One of God." But Jesus rebuked him, saying, "Be silent, and come out of him!" And the unclean spirit, convulsing him and crying with a loud voice, came out of him. They were all amazed, and they kept on asking one another, "What is this? A new teaching—with authority! He commands even the unclean spirits, and they obey him" (1:23–27).

Whatever modern medical science might judge an "unclean spirit" to be, the point here is Jesus' power and authority. It is not by accident that an "unclean spirit"—whose self-identification is in the first person plural, "us," further heightening the bizarre nature of the event—is the first in the Gospel of Mark to recognize and announce Jesus' identity. For Jesus comes to destroy evil and rob death of its victory. With six words, Jesus deprives the unclean spirit of its power over the man, and right away everyone recognizes, to their amazement, that something new is happening in this man Jesus.

Notice, in this story it is a man who has an unclean spirit. What man has not sometimes felt that he was in the grip of an unclean spirit, something he would rather be rid of? The power of popular culture, with its phony images of what it means to be a man, could certainly be called an "unclean spirit." Mark's Gospel presents Jesus as the one who has power to banish unclean spirits. Is this not a Jesus any man can respect and want to have as a close friend?

Chapter 3

A Catholic Man's Approach to the Scriptures

IS IT POSSIBLE that a man's approach to Scripture is different from a woman's? Surprising as it may be, the answer is yes. As psychologist Laura Schlessinger, Ph.D., has written, "Men are never going to be just like women. Nor should they try to be. What is unique to each individual should be given respect and opportunity. What is more natural and comfortable to each gender ought to be given equal respect and opportunity."[1]

Dr. Schlessinger goes on to explain that for men, expressing emotions "is perhaps less central, though not less essential," than it is for women. Men tend to be "more 'action' and 'external' oriented" than women. "Human males have always had a typically restless attitude about new adventure, exploit, challenge, battle, etc."[2] So it is not surprising that men and women would relate to God's word in differing ways.

Generally speaking, men approach the Scriptures from more of an action-oriented perspective. They want to know, for example, what Jesus *does,* and they want to know about the practical implications of Jesus' words. Men might ask, How can I live out what Jesus models or teaches? For men, the emphasis is on what it means to "do" Christian faith, so that is what they tend to look for in Scripture. Men are also interested in questions of meaning and in relational issues, but they tend to focus more on "how to do" the message of the gospel. They are interested in observing and learning from Jesus' feelings as portrayed by the gospels, but awareness leads more to action questions than to a consideration of Jesus' emotions.

Catholic men should be able to read the New Testament and return to it endlessly for new inspiration and insight. Jesus is male, and the gospels and the other New Testament documents have no shortage of male characters. Additionally, Jesus' preferred metaphor for God is *Abba,* usually translated "Father," but "loving Papa" is more accurate; and the Bible overwhelmingly prefers male metaphors and pronouns for God. Not only that, but despite the lack of clarity about the exact human authorship of the gospels, few if any scholars would doubt that men carried out the redaction process. With such a heavy male influence on the gospels, men should find it easy to read and draw spiritual nourishment from them. Yet in our culture women do most of the Bible purchasing and reading. Our culture has so little respect for men as spiritual and religious beings that relatively few men steep themselves in Scripture and draw from that well the masculine spiritual vitality to be found there.

This is particularly true for Catholic men because Catholicism does not so deeply distrust the popular culture as evangelical and fundamentalist Christian churches do. Catholicism is committed to being in and for the world, but "not of" the world. Sometimes, however, Catholics overlook the "not of" dimension of their faith because the "in" and "for" thrust of Catholicism is so prominent. Because Catholicism looks for

God in popular culture as it does almost everywhere else, Catholic men are heavily influenced by current cultural values, particularly by the popular culture's discomfort with male religious behavior. Hence the male Catholic's discomfort with being "religious" in general and with being on intimate terms with the Scriptures.[3] This despite the fact that the Bible is saturated with testosterone, if you will. Men who read and pray with Scripture place themselves at risk, in our culture, of compromising their masculinity.

Ironically, instead of drawing nourishment for a male faith from the Bible's masculine perspectives, Catholic men who do accept the importance of Scripture—and this includes both clergy and laity—often take up the banner of Catholic feminism. Whenever a Catholic feminist waxes indignant about the heavy male character of the Scriptures, men sympathetic to feminist issues chant, "Yes, yes, we're offended, too," and support the attempt to make the Bible texts gender neutral. Not only do they support translations of Scripture that introduce inclusive language with regard to people—a perfectly justifiable step since there are both male and female human beings, and the intended meaning of the term "man" or "men" refers to both sexes. But they also support Bible translations that alter the predominance of masculine pronouns and male metaphors for God—a step that has questionable value since God is beyond gender, and the scriptural documents are historically and culturally conditioned, whether we like it or not.

With regard to liturgical texts, this approach either substitutes gender-neutral language—inserting "God" wherever a masculine pronoun for the deity occurs, for example, thus banishing a personal God from the liturgy—or introduces a more-or-less equal balance of feminine and masculine pronouns and metaphors for God. On the level of metaphor, only constant mental gymnastics spare us an androgynous God, a mixed metaphor with no basis in actual human experience, since there is no such being as an "androgyne."

Given the contemporary cultural climate, it is perfectly possible for Catholic men to understand Catholic women's offense at male metaphors and masculine pronouns for God. Whether women are justified in taking offense is debatable, however, as is the charge that using nothing but masculine metaphors and pronouns for God means men are more like God than women are. Still, the objection is sincere, and men need to take it seriously. Catholic men need to acknowledge that the Bible's heavily male perspective is nothing to boast about and is not to be used to uphold lack of equality between men and women, in the Church or in the world.

The preponderance of male perspectives, characters, and metaphors in the Bible is simply an objective historical and cultural fact. One dares to suggest that women offended by this are just as out of line as men who would try to base male superiority on it. The Bible is heavily male in its origins and makeup, but with few exceptions the New Testament embodies remarkably egalitarian perspectives with regard to women. There it is.

The open, accepting, countercultural attitude of Jesus toward women in the gospels, particularly Mark and John, should carry considerable weight for men who read the Bible. Men can draw on Jesus' example, nourishing a healthy male spirituality without relegating women to a second-class status. For women, an equally balanced and healthy perspective on Scripture that does not depend upon trying to eliminate their historically and culturally conditioned character is possible. Such a perspective need not depend upon an arrogant rewriting of biblical documents to bring them into line with a contemporary feminist ideology.

It is possible that in the long run it will be better for both men and women if Catholics resist the feminist ideological demand for an androgynous God. Perhaps, as Scripture scholar John W. Miller persuasively argues, a "monotheistic father religion" is psychologically and theologically preferable for both men and women.[4]

The rest of this chapter will take for granted that historically and culturally the gospels are "saturated with testosterone." It will also help male Catholic readers take advantage of this quality for their own spiritual well-being. At the same time, we will be sure to point out how the gospels dispel any basis for concluding that the humanity of women is inferior to that of men. Neither this book nor its author would support any attempt to use the masculine character of the Scriptures to promote female subservience to men or female inferiority in the Church.

Returning to where we left off with the Gospel of Mark in chapter 2: following the synagogue scene, Mark informs us that because of Jesus' astonishing debut as a teacher, his fame began to grow throughout the region of Galilee. Jesus pays no attention to this, however, instead moving directly to the home of Simon's mother-in-law:

> Now Simon's mother-in-law was in bed with a fever, and they told him about her at once. He came and took her by the hand and lifted her up. Then the fever left her, and she began to serve them (1:30–31).

Notice, one of the first miracles Jesus performs in Mark's Gospel is a curing miracle, and the subject is a woman. Is this a mere coincidence? Perhaps, but keep in mind that the human redactors of the gospels virtually never do anything without a specific theological purpose in mind. If the first miracle Jesus performs is the cure of a woman with a fever, it is because Mark's Gospel wants to say something about Jesus and about the faith of the Christian community.

A group of men—Simon and Andrew, James and John—alert Jesus to the fact that the mother of Simon's wife needs his attention. Had Jesus, and Mark, wanted to promote male superiority, it would have made sense for Jesus' first miracles to focus on men only. Instead, following the first public proclamation of his message, Jesus' concerns include the needs of a woman, whom he cures of "a fever."

Clearly, Jesus sees nothing unmasculine in caring for and serving a woman. Why did the redactor of Mark present this account so early in his gospel? Perhaps he wanted to show, up front, that the man Jesus did not discriminate in his attitudes. He has just chosen four men as his first disciples, true. But his care and concern for women is without question, and he shows no sign of condescension. At the very least, Jesus' example suggests to Catholic men today that their attention to women, and their relationships with women, to be Christlike, must have an egalitarian foundation. A "real man" does not relegate women to a second-class status. Whether in marriage or in professional or ministerial relationships, mutual respect is the order of the day, every day.

Following the cure of Simon's mother-in-law, apparently word of the miracle spreads quickly. Soon the whole town knows about it. Jesus becomes even more active:

> That evening, at sundown, they brought to him all who were sick or possessed with demons. And the whole city was gathered around the door. And he cured many who were sick with various diseases, and cast out many de-

mons; and he would not permit the demons to speak, because they knew him.

In the morning, while it was still very dark, he got up and went out to a deserted place, and there he prayed (1:32–35).

Jesus has a day of teaching in the synagogue, followed by much human interaction and the curing of "many who were sick," not to mention the casting out of "demons." Note that according to Mark's Gospel, Jesus forbids the demons from speaking "because they knew him." Jesus recognizes and controls evil—personified here as "demons"—when he encounters it. In the face of the demonic, the man Jesus is unmovable and uncompromising.

It is easy to read a brief gospel account such as this one and miss the power, even the violence, of its message. The Jesus of this passage is a man with an iron glint in his eye, and Catholic men learn from him that the forces of evil have no rights. Care for others, an active concern for those with special needs, is central to Christian discipleship—doing as Jesus did, bringing his influence into the present moment under whatever circumstances. At the same time, opposition from the powers of darkness, in whatever form, should come as no surprise. Assertive persistence, in union with the risen Christ, will enable right and good to triumph because, ultimately, evil is powerless.

At this point in his narrative, with deceptive simplicity, Mark drops in a line about Jesus that has tremendous implications for a Christian understanding of Jesus' masculinity. "In the morning, while it was still very dark," Mark says, "[Jesus] got up and went out to a deserted place, and there he prayed" (1:35).

It is impossible to overemphasize the importance of this sentence, especially coming so early in the first gospel written.

Thirty-four verses into the Gospel of Mark, we watch as Jesus rises before dawn. Yesterday was filled with activity, so he must have been exhausted. Still, he opens his eyes, rises from sleep, and makes his way to "a deserted place," a place where he can be alone with God. Mark could not be more plainspoken. "There he prayed," Mark says. We don't know how long it was before "Simon and his companions" came looking for Jesus, but it could have been two or three hours. Even if it was only one hour, Jesus spent a significant amount of time in solitary prayer. Clearly, this was important to him. It was a priority.

We have no reason to believe that this was a first-time experience for Jesus. The idea of going off by himself to pray did not just suddenly strike him this morning. The Jesus who rises before dawn to be alone with God in prayer is a man who developed the habit of solitary prayer years ago, as a young man, perhaps even as a boy. The male author of Mark, as well as the faith community he represents, holds the oral tradition about Jesus' dedication to solitary prayer in high esteem. Otherwise, this mention of Jesus' solitary prayer would not appear in the Gospel of Mark.

Jesus the man was devoted to solitary prayer. The dominant male perspective of Mark's Gospel passes this devotion along to the disciples of Jesus down through history to our own day. It is an important part of being a man. A "real man," a man who would follow Jesus and live his Christian faith in today's world, will with Jesus courageously devote himself to becoming a prayerful person. Just as Jesus makes a personal sacrifice by rising before dawn to be alone with his Father, today's Catholic man will make whatever sacrifices are necessary to be alone with his Father in prayer.

As Mark's Gospel continues, Jesus shows a preference for mission over human interaction:

And Simon and his companions hunted for him. When they found him, they said to him, "Everyone is searching for you." He answered, "Let us go on to the neighboring towns, so that I may proclaim the message there also; for that is what I came out to do." And he went throughout Galilee, proclaiming the message in their synagogues and casting out demons (1:36–39).

When Simon and the others finally track him down, they urge Jesus to return with them to enjoy the adulation of his new disciples—to be a celebrity. Instead, he insists that they move on to other towns where he can "proclaim the message." This, Jesus insists, is what he is here for. This is his purpose, and he will not be distracted. Mark tells us that this is precisely what Jesus does, "proclaiming the message in their synagogues and casting out demons."

Mark's Jesus understands himself not as "a people person" but as "a mission person." His main concern is to proclaim the good news of God's unconditional love, the need for conversion, and the coming of the reign of God. He is a man of action, and "casting out demons" is a visible manifestation of the beginning eruption of God's kingdom in human history.

When he is with people, the male Jesus prefers "doing" over "being." It is when he is alone with his Father that Jesus balances "doing" with "being." Jesus is active when he is with people, contemplative when he turns to solitary prayer. Nothing could manifest Jesus' maleness more clearly.

Catholic men can take inspiration and encouragement from Jesus when they find themselves more action-oriented in their everyday life and in their Church-life. It is perfectly natural and Christlike for men to "do" their faith more than to reflect on it or talk about it. Most of the time, men simply do not prefer to spend as much energy on reflecting and talking as they do on acting out their faith. Especially in our culture, men need to take seriously the example of Jesus the contemplative. Catholic men need to set aside times for prayer, silent retreats, and days of recollection. But like the man Jesus, most of the time most men will be more inclined to action than to contemplation. The traditional Benedictine motto is *"ora et labora"* ("pray and work"). Even men who live in monasteries frequently appreciate the *labora* part of their life at least as much as the *ora* part. The point, however, is not that the two are mutually exclusive. Rather, it is a matter of emphasis, and Jesus shows men how to balance the active with the contemplative.

Mark next tells us about an encounter between Jesus and a man with leprosy. Pay close attention to exactly how Jesus and the afflicted man interact with each other:

> A leper came to him begging him, and kneeling he said to him, "If you choose, you can make me clean." Moved with pity, Jesus stretched out his hand and touched him, and said to him, "I do choose. Be made clean!" Immediately the leprosy left him, and he was made clean. After sternly warning him he sent him away at once, saying to him, "See that you say nothing to anyone; but go, show yourself to the priest, and offer for your cleansing what Moses commanded, as a testimony to them." But he went out and began to proclaim it freely, and to spread the word, so that Jesus could no longer go into a town openly, but stayed out in the country; and people came to him from every quarter (1:40–45).

To begin with, Mark tells us about Jesus' emotions in this situation. He is "moved with pity." In reading this line, men will probably find this fact of interest. Jesus feels pity. Intriguing. But a man is unlikely to dwell on it. A female reader is likely to be more deeply impressed by Mark's comment on Jesus' feelings. A woman is likely to be fascinated and to want to ponder the statement at some length, may even want to meditate on it and discuss it with others. There's nothing objectionable about this; it's just not the response a male reader is most likely to have.

A male reader is inclined to be more in tune with Mark himself as he moves along with his narrative. His comment about Jesus' feelings is simply a prefatory observation at the beginning of the sentence. This is how Jesus felt when the man with leprosy spoke to him asking to be cured, but here is what Jesus *did* about it.

Jesus does not set the example for Saint Francis of Assisi, who dramatically embraced and kissed a leper early in the process of his conversion some eleven centuries later. Rather, Jesus simply reaches out and touches the man. On his head? on his shoulder? on his face? Mark does not say. Had a woman been the redactor of Mark, she would have been inclined to say exactly where Jesus touched the man with leprosy because such a personal detail would have been important to her. Jesus stretched out his hand and touched him on his face…arm…hand. But the redactor of Mark, a man, is not interested in *where* Jesus touched the man, only *that* Jesus touched him.

Instantly, the nameless man is cured of his leprosy, and Jesus' next move is a characteristically male one. No doubt, the man is grateful to Jesus for curing him, but neither he nor Jesus make a big deal out of it. They do not embrace and weep with joy. This is not the beginning of a beautiful friendship. Instead, Jesus sends the man away "at once," and he "sternly" warns him to keep quiet about what has happened. Jesus tells the man to follow the dictates of the Jewish Law. Follow the rules, Jesus insists.

The man Jesus cured is not inclined to follow directions, however—which is also not atypical of men. Instead, he "went out and began to proclaim it freely, and to spread the word." The redactor of Mark clearly intends this language of proclamation and word to evoke the spirit of evangelization. The man cured of leprosy is a model for believers, and their response to Jesus' gift of salvation—spiritual liberation and healing—should be similar to that of the fortunate man. In particular, male readers of Mark should recognize that a man goes off and proclaims the word himself.

Next, following the cure of a paralyzed man and the cure of a man with a withered hand, we read Mark's account of how Jesus chose the men who were to be his apostles:

> He went up the mountain and called to him those whom he wanted, and they came to him. And he appointed twelve, whom he also named apostles, to be with him, and to be sent out to proclaim the message, and to have authority to cast out demons. So he appointed the twelve: Simon (to whom he gave the name Peter); James son of Zebedee and John the brother of James (to whom he gave the name Boanerges, that is, Sons of Thunder); and Andrew, and Philip, and Bartholomew, and Matthew, and Thomas, and James son of Alphaeus, and Thaddaeus, and Simon the Cananaean, and Judas Iscariot, who betrayed him (3:13–19).

All of Jesus' apostles are men. Culturally conditioned as this choice no doubt was, and culturally conditioned as Mark's account of it no doubt is, all the same there is no reason men should not take inspiration from the fact that Jesus surrounded himself with men. What feminist interpreters do with this fact is another matter, but men are free to take from it encouragement to make Christian discipleship foundational to what it means to be a man. Jesus chooses men "to be with him, and to be sent out to proclaim the message, and to have authority to cast out demons." And Judas, one of the men Jesus chose, turns out to be a rat.

Catholic men are free to approach the Scriptures with a conscious awareness that the Scriptures are "saturated with testosterone." The Bible is not meant to be a resource for wimps. "Indeed, the word of God is living and active, sharper than any two-edged sword, piercing until it divides soul from spirit, joints from marrow..." (Hebrews 4:12)—a powerful, masculine image if ever there was one. Regardless of how women may read the Scriptures, men may tap into the sacred writings as a lifeline for a masculine spirituality and need not apologize to women for doing so. From this experience men should be able to find endless nourishment for a genuinely masculine spirituality.

Chapter 4
A Catholic Man's Approach to the Sacraments

IF THERE IS anything that makes Catholicism unique it is its sacraments, these seven visible carriers of an invisible reality: baptism, confirmation, Eucharist, reconciliation, matrimony, holy orders, and anointing of the sick. "The sacraments," says the *Catechism of the Catholic Church*,

> are efficacious signs of grace, instituted by Christ and entrusted to the Church, by which divine life is dispensed to us. The visible rites by which the sacraments are celebrated signify and make present the graces proper to each sacrament. They bear fruit in those who receive them with the required dispositions (No. 1131).

Each sacrament is a way to actively nourish our relationship with Christ and with his people, the Church. Catholic men tend to approach each of the sacraments as an *action*, as something one *does*. In other words, the sacraments are not meditations in which we are passive recipients; they are communal, sensate encounters with the risen Christ that require our active involvement. The sacraments utilize created and human realities: water and the spoken word, bread and wine, words of forgiveness and gestures, blessings and anointing with oil, the committed personal intimacy of husband and wife, the laying on of hands by a bishop, and prayers for healing coupled with anointing with blessed oil. In the sacraments, we touch Christ and he touches us. This active mutuality holds particular appeal for men.

The male approach to the sacraments is perhaps best compared to the way two men approach friendship with each other. They most often enjoy each other's companionship by participating in a shared activity or project—anything from sports to playing musical instruments, from computer-related activities to mechanical projects. Men who are friends would rather go fishing together than sit in a coffee shop and talk. Most often, that's how men go about being friends. In comparison, women who are friends enjoy simply being with one another and talking at length about themselves, their relationships, their work, and their lives in general. Men support and encourage one another not so much by talking and giving hugs—although they do this sometimes, too—as by "being there" for one another and by offering practical assistance in problem solving.

In a humorous vein, the outdoors humor essays in the books of Patrick F. McManus constitute a fine illustration. McManus is a gifted writer and a Catholic. While religion rarely surfaces explicitly in his stories, all the same his male Catholic sensibilities are entirely active as he tells hilarious stories of his boyhood adventures and misadventures in books such as *The Night the Bear Ate Goombaw* and *Into the Wilderness, Endlessly Grousing*.[1] In his stories, Pat McManus's male characters—

A Catholic Man's Approach to the Sacraments

Rancid Crabtree, Eddie Muldoon, and Retch Sweeney among the most popular—do not "share," they engage in shared activities. They learn about life and the world by interacting with life and the world together. This is the male approach to life and the world.

If I need some electrical wiring done in my house, my friend who knows more about electrical work than I do shows his friendship by helping me do the work and helping to solve problems that arise in the course of the project. When the work is done, we are closer friends than we were before. If we are characters in a Pat McManus story, we have also had an amusing adventure—amusing to our readers, at least. This is not to say that all examples of shared male activity must be of a "blue-collar" nature. Two men who are teachers, investment counselors, writers, engineers, artists, computer programmers, or computer technicians will share projects related to their work or avocations.

In a similar way, Catholic men approach the sacraments as ways to go about being friends with Christ. Ordinarily, men think of their relationship with Christ as something that expresses itself in action. They are "with Christ" by doing things with and for him and by asking him to help them to be faithful to their commitments, to complete projects they work on, and so forth.

Sometimes men need and want to simply "be with" Christ, while praying, making a silent retreat, or experiencing a day of recollection. "Being with" Jesus is a crucial element of any Christian faith. But most commonly, men live their faith by *acting on* their faith. Men live their faith by being faithful to their commitments, by working, and by helping others. In a very real sense, the sacraments are a blend of both "being" and "doing." A sacrament is both an action and a way to "be with"

Christ in a particular set of circumstances with a specific purpose in mind. A sacrament might be described, from a male perspective, as an action that expresses a mode of being, namely, living one's life as a disciple of Christ.

There is a remarkable scene in novelist James Lee Burke's *Heaven's Prisoners*. Burke is a Catholic—one reviewer called him "the Graham Greene of the bayou"—and his main character, Dave Robicheaux, lives in New Iberia Parish, Louisiana. Dave saves a little Salvadoran girl from drowning when the airplane she is in with her mother crashes in a bayou near Dave's home. Later, when the little girl asks, in Spanish, where her mother is, Dave and his wife, Annie, take the little girl, whom they name Alafair, to their parish church. There they try to communicate with the girl in a mixture of English, French, Spanish, and ritual:

> She didn't ask what had happened to her mother; she asked instead where she had gone. So we drove her to St. Peter's Church in New Iberia. I suppose one might say that my attempt at resolution was facile. But I believe that ritual and metaphor exist for a reason. Words have no governance over either birth or death, and they never make the latter more acceptable, no matter how many times its inevitability is explained to us. We each held her hand and walked her up the aisle of the empty church to the scrolled metal stand of burning candles that stood before statues of Mary, Joseph, and the infant Jesus.
>
> "*Ta maman est avec Jésus,*" I said to her in French. "*Au ciel.*"
>
> Her face was round, and her eyes blinked at me.
>
> "*Cielo?*" she asked.
>
> "Yes, in the sky. *Au ciel,*" I said.

"*En el cielo*," Annie said. "In heaven."
Alafair's face was perplexed as she at first looked back and forth between us, then I saw her lips purse and her eyes start to water.
"Hey, hey, little guy," I said, and picked her up on my hip. "Come on, I want you to light a candle. *Pour ta maman.*"
I lit the punk on a burning candle, put it in her hand, and helped her touch it to a dead wick inside a red glass candle container. She watched the teardrop of fire rise off the wax, then I moved her hand and the lighted punk to another wick and then another.[2]

James Lee Burke understands the Catholic sacramental sensibility from a distinctively male perspective. He knows that "ritual and metaphor exist for a reason." He knows that sacraments—or in this case sacramental devotional gestures—are ways to "be with" and respond to life's mysteries, in this case death. Dave Robicheaux copes with the little girl's anxiety about her mother's whereabouts in a typically Catholic male fashion. He tells her the truth, and he does something about it. Words alone are insufficient. Words coupled with ritual and metaphor are better.

Lighting candles and similar pious practices are natural developments in the context of the Catholic sacramental imagination. Because we have the seven sacraments, which are a blend of ritual and metaphor that actually give what they say they give, we naturally develop other "sacramental" ways of expressing and nourishing our faith. Lighting candles, burning incense, sprinkling holy water, blessing ourselves and others with the sign of the cross, all are natural extensions of the Catholic sacramental sensibility. All are ways of "doing something" relative to a sacred moment in human existence, and because they are actions, men can be comfortable with them.

Could we not say the same as far as Catholic women are concerned? Yes. And no. Psychologically, there is a subtle but important difference. Women are more inclined to relate to the sacraments as personal interactions with Christ rather than as shared activities. For a woman, a sacrament emphasizes being rather than doing. For a man, a sacrament is something Christ, and the community, and I do together. It's a shared activity, which emphasizes doing rather than being. For both men and women, of course, both being and doing are part of the experience. It's a matter of perspective, and the male perspective is somewhat different from that of women.

This subtle difference between how men and women experience the sacraments is important for those in liturgical ministries to keep in mind. Women tend to want liturgies that emphasize aesthetics and human interaction. Men appreciate aesthetic values and the human element in liturgy, of course, but the experience will be incomplete for a man if aesthetics and human interaction overwhelm the theological substance of the liturgy. A man is more comfortable with a liturgy in which it is clear that the community faces God together in a stance of direct worship, rather than filtering the liturgy heavily through human interactions of various kinds. In Jungian terms, a man in touch with his feminine side appreciates aesthetics and human interactions in liturgy, but his dominant masculinity leads him to worship God directly. A woman in touch with her masculine side appreciates direct worship of God, but her dominant femininity craves liturgical aesthetics and liturgical human interaction.

As things stand in the Church today, women tend to have more influence in liturgical situations because women active in parishes outnumber men who are active in parishes, plus women can wave the banner of female oppression and patriarchal prejudice. What women sometimes do not understand is that the mere presence of an all-male clergy counts for virtually nothing as far as most men are concerned. The sanctuary can be filled with male clergy, and the liturgy itself can be almost entirely feminized. In some parish Masses, for example, the custom as the congregation prays the Our Father is for everyone to hold hands. Wherever this chummy practice originated, it is highly unlikely that it was a man's idea.

Progressive Catholic males, both clerical and lay, do not want to be perceived as antifeminist, so they frequently bow to pressures from women to feminize the liturgy. This means they must repress their natural male inclination toward direct, simple communal worship of God. For their part, women are sometimes so angry about an all-male clergy and about patriarchalism in the Church that they repress their masculine side, which appreciates direct worship of God. This means that the liturgy becomes feminized in a way that is unbalanced and unhealthy for both women and men.

Ideally, masculine and feminine approaches to liturgy would be in balance, both sexes respecting the other's spiritual and liturgical needs. Ideally, liturgies would be both aesthetically appealing with regard to music, worship space, and interior decoration, and would offer appropriate opportunities for liturgical human interaction. At the same time, a liturgy would have a significant, noticeable focus on the direct worship of God. That is, the liturgy would simply "do" the Eucharist "by the book" and limit hand-holding, highly demonstrative sharings of the sign of peace, and so forth.

Another way to express this male/female difference and complementarity is to do so in terms of transcendence and immanence. The dominant male inclination is to focus on the transcendence of God, while the dominant female inclination is to appreciate God's immanence. For men, God is transcendent to the point of immanence; for women, God is immanent to the point of transcendence.

These terms help to explain one reason why Catholic women are sometimes more irritated by noninclusive religious language than men. Women "feel" religious language more intimately than men. Because for men God is first of all transcendent, men are indifferent to religious language—until women bring it to men's attention, of course, which puts the issue in men's faces, and it then becomes an immediate issue, indeed. Dialogue between men and women then becomes important, and the issue of infallibility enters the picture, too. Both men and women frequently act as if they could never be mistaken in their respective positions. One of the remarks one virtually never hears in discussions of inclusive language and other feminist issues in the Church is "I could be wrong."

This does not mean that men cannot perceive or appreciate God's immanence, and it does not mean that women cannot appreciate God's transcendence. Once again, it's a simple matter of dominant inclination. The extent to which this model fails to provide a satisfactory explanation, of course, is the extent to which the popular Jungian *anima/animus* theory falls short of reality.

These observations on the unique ways men and women approach the sacraments apply not only to eucharistic liturgies but to celebrations of all the sacraments. Men think of sacraments, primarily, as ritual activities that lead them to Christ and nourish their journey with Christ. Women think of sacraments, primarily, as interpersonal encounters with Christ. Now for a closer look, from a male perspective, at the two sacraments that are most basic to a Catholic man's life and faith.

Baptism

The *Catechism of the Catholic Church* describes baptism as "birth into the new life in Christ" (1277). Baptism is the first of the three sacraments of initiation, the others being confirmation and Eucharist. The essential elements of the baptismal ritual are the pouring of water over the person's forehead, or the immersing of the person in a pool of water, coupled with the recitation of the traditional baptismal formula as directed by Jesus in the Gospel of Matthew (28:19): "I baptize you in the name of the Father, and of the Son, and of the Holy Spirit."

From a male perspective, the baptismal ritual is an action the community carries out on behalf of the person being baptized and an action the person engages in relative to Christ and the community of faith, which is the Body of Christ. Men also approach baptism as the key to understanding the Christian life. Baptism is the beginning of a lifelong personal interaction with Christ. The ritual itself is soon over and done with, so what becomes significant over the long haul is how the grace of baptism influences the rest of that person's life in Christ. This is a predominantly practical point of view, even though baptism, like all the sacraments, is a mystical experience.

Probably the most significant scriptural commentary on the meaning of baptism comes from Saint Paul, in his Letter to the Romans:

> Do you not know that all of us who have been baptized into Christ Jesus were baptized into his death? Therefore we have been buried with him by baptism into death, so that, just as Christ was raised from the dead by the glory of the Father, so we too might walk in newness of life.
> For if we have been united with him in a death like his,

we will certainly be united with him in a resurrection like his (6:3–5).

Paul explains baptism in a practical manner. Through baptism we share mystically and actually in the death and Resurrection of Jesus. We share in the effects of his death and Resurrection as well. As Paul says in another place, "I have been crucified with Christ; and it is no longer I who live, but it is Christ who lives in me. And the life I now live in the flesh I live by faith in the Son of God, who loved me and gave himself for me" (Galatians 2:19b–20).

A man reading words such as these from Saint Paul will want to know about the practical implications. If we share in the effects of the death and Resurrection of Christ, what does that mean here and now, in my everyday life? What does it mean for my relationships with other people, for the work I do, for how I spend my time and money? If baptism has no practical implications "in the real world," then what's the point? If baptism has no real consequences in my everyday life, then baptism is little more than an empty pious ritual.

For a man, baptism shifts the focus of his daily life away from self toward God and other people. There is nothing original about this insight, and we would need to make the identical observation if we were talking about women. They, too, must say with Saint Paul that "it is no longer I who live, but it is Christ who lives in me." For men, however, the practical consequences, in our culture, take on a particular shape and direction. The shift in focus is away from an unfettered, shapeless, directionless existence toward a life given shape and character by permanent commitments. Just as Christ makes a permanent, unconditional commitment to us, so as Christ lives in each one of us we are to live out our Christian identity by doing the same.

For most men, this means marriage and fatherhood. For some Catholic men, their baptism will find expression in the ordained celibate priesthood.

Another quality of baptism is that it is the most basic sacrament of Christian identity, and for a man the identification of himself with Christ will include not only a sense of Christ living in him. It will also include living in close companionship with Christ. This means that Christ will be with us in being faithful to the commitments we make. To use the example of marriage again: the primary focus of a man who marries is no longer professional success—important as this may remain to him—or anything else but success in marriage. This requires a major shift from self-centeredness to other-centeredness, and Christ's companionship is central to a man's ability to make this shift, to place love of God and neighbor (wife, children, family) at the center of his existence.

For most men, marriage goes hand-in-hand with fatherhood, and this is also a permanent commitment. At the same time, being a good father does not happen automatically. "It is easier for a father to have children," said Pope John XXIII, "than for children to have a real father."[3]

When we marry, and when we have children, we focus our lives in specific directions. We make a commitment to prioritize our lives with our marriage and our children at the top of the list. Everything else comes second, including our work, our hobbies, and even volunteer activities in our parish or elsewhere. Sometimes men seem to have a natural inclination to dissociate themselves from family relationships, to "escape" into work or other activities outside the home and away from family life. One of the main consequences of taking one's baptism seriously, however, is the firm determination to resist this inclination in order to give our time, our very self, to spouse and children.

This is what they want and need, far more than anything else we can give them.

Eucharist

The Eucharist, or Mass, is traditionally called the "summit and source" of life in the Catholic community. "The Sunday celebration of the Lord's Day and his Eucharist," says the *Catechism of the Catholic Church,* "is at the heart of the Church's life" (2177).

Attending Mass and receiving holy Communion is critically important for Catholic men for two reasons. First, men consciously need to cultivate a sense of belonging to and being active in a parish. Sometimes men feel a tug toward an unhealthy form of independence and self-sufficiency. We live in a culture that not only encourages men to be "loners" but also denies the spirituality of men and their inherent religious nature—the emptiness in the male heart that only God can satisfy. Participation at least on Sundays in the communal liturgical life of a parish is an ideal way to resist the ease of independence and to reject the popular cultural notion that spirituality and religion are for weaklings and geeks. On the contrary, it takes considerable courage and maturity to embrace Christian faith and live a conspicuously Catholic life day in, day out.

Second, in our era it is theologically unfashionable to view a sacrament as a "source of grace." Yet this is a legitimate perspective, one that can be particularly helpful for many men who think in concrete terms. Contemporary theology understands the term *grace* to refer to God's gift of his own divine life to us, and this is what we mean when we say that a sacrament "gives grace." To participate in the Mass, and receive holy Communion, is to nourish oneself at the fountain of divine life. For a man to do this is to cultivate a deeper intimacy with the risen Christ and to open himself more and more to Christ's influence and guidance. There is nothing "magical" about this; it is simply a matter of a man becoming what he beholds.

Many, perhaps most, men would find it impossible to attend Mass more than once a week, on Sunday morning or Saturday evening. Still, with work schedules becoming more flexible for some men, they may find it possible to receive holy Communion more often, perhaps even daily. Men who are able to do this often report that once they establish a habit of daily Mass, their day seems incomplete without it.

Men today sometimes find themselves unsure of what the Eucharist means, why it should be so important. Sometimes they wonder about the actual meaning of the Mass. In the Eucharist we receive both the scriptural word of God and the body and blood of Christ, "body and blood, soul and divinity." Simply to repeat the traditional formula, however, may not "work" for many men today. Keep in mind that *body and blood* is a Semitic phrase that means "the whole person." Nothing more, nothing less. So in the Eucharist we receive the "whole person" of Christ. In addition, we receive not the "whole person" of the historical man, Jesus. Holy Communion is not a mysterious spiritual "blast from the past." Rather, we receive the "whole person" of *the risen Christ,* as he exists now, today, alive and active in the Church and in the world. This is a great mystery!

Why is this important? Regular, even frequent participation in the Mass is important for a man because by it he is nourished from the inside out by the risen Christ. Thus, a man nourishes his fully human, fully spiritual communion with the one who is at the heart of his existence as a man. Participation in the Eucharist helps a man enormously when it comes to staying "in tune" with the Lord Jesus on every level of his being.

For a Catholic man, the sacraments are actions that serve as a source of eternal life and divine grace. A man experiences the sacraments as ways to nourish friendship with Christ and a healthy, balanced life in this world. Far from being "magic moments," the sacraments are sacred activities a man shares with the risen Lord and with his people, the Church. The sacraments are what enable a Catholic man to "put flesh on" his faith.

Chapter 5

A Catholic Man's Approach to Family Life

FAMILY LIFE IS, for most Catholic men, the usual place they find themselves. It is in the context of family relationships that a boy grows into manhood, and it is in the context of marriage and family life that most men live out their faith and discover their deepest identity. Family life is where men meet their greatest challenges, experience their deepest anguishes, and find their deepest joys. From a Catholic theological perspective, family life is at the very heart of the Church's life. Therefore, a Catholic "family man" is intimately involved with the Church in its most basic form.

Some history and theology will be helpful. Pope John Paul II has made it clear on numerous occasions that the family—and we need to add "in its various forms"—is the foundational unit of the Church. The parish is not the Church's bottom line, the family is. A parish is made up of households, most of which are families of various shapes and sizes. If faith is not alive and thriving in those families—and we're not talking about rampant superficial piety here—then faith grows weaker at the parish level. It's as simple as that. The remarks of Pope John Paul II during his September 1987 visit to the United States are relevant:

> ...the family itself is the first and most appropriate place for teaching the truths of the faith, the practice of Christian virtues and the essential values of human life.
>
> ...every parish is *a family of families*. The vitality of a parish greatly depends on the spiritual vigor, commitment and involvement of its families. The family in fact is the basic unit of society and of the Church. It is "the domestic Church." Families are those living cells which come together to form the very substance of parish life.[1]

But where does this line of thought come from? John Paul II did not dream it up one day on a walk around the Vatican gardens, that's for sure. This insight goes back as far as Christianity's Jewish roots. When the first Christians gathered for worship, after they were ejected from the synagogues, they met in one another's homes. Even today, in the Jewish tradition, it is the home, around the family table, where the most significant religious rituals and events are celebrated. Jewish author Arlene Rossen Cardozo writes, "For centuries the family has been the means through which traditional Jewish celebrations have survived and flourished."[2]

In the late fourth century, in his commentaries on Genesis and the Letter to the Ephesians, Saint John Chrysostom called the family *ekklesia,* the New Testament term for "church." A few times he used the diminutive form *ekklesiola* ("little church"), but most often he simply called the family "church."[3]

This insight was all but lost in the wake of the Protestant

Reformation and the Catholic Counter-Reformation. The Council of Trent (1545–1563), for example, placed the responsibility for the religious formation of children on the shoulders of the parish priest. Hence the feeling of many parents today that they are incompetent when it comes to the religious education of their own children.

In the late nineteenth century Pope Leo XIII wrote that "the family was ordained of God.... It was before the Church, or rather the first form of the Church on earth." Leo's reminder was largely ignored, unfortunately, until the Second Vatican Council in the mid-1960s. But both of this latest Council's major documents on the Church called the family "the domestic Church." Later, in his 1975 apostolic exhortation on evangelization, Pope Paul VI declared, "There should be found in every family the various aspects of the entire Church." And in 1980, at the Mass that opened the international synod of bishops, Pope John Paul II said that the family is meant to "constitute the Church in its fundamental dimension."

Clearly, the insight that the family, or household, is the most basic unit of the Church is firmly rooted in Catholic tradition. And when the risen Christ, in the Gospel of Matthew, says, "Where two or three are gathered in my name, I am there among them" (18:20), there is no question that we may apply these words to family life. Any Catholic man involved in a family is, therefore, involved in the life of the Church at its most fundamental level. Men and Church leaders at all levels must take this observation seriously. To accuse men who are not volunteering hours a week for their parish of not being "active in the Church" is shortsighted at best. This does not mean that men should feel no responsibility to their parish. It does mean that a man's family comes first.

For most Catholic men, the sacrament at the heart of their

baptismal commitment, and their Church membership, is marriage. A married man goes about being a disciple of Christ first of all by being married. Indeed, for a Catholic man, his relationship with his spouse is inseparable from his relationship with Christ. In the Gospel of Luke, Jesus says, "You shall love the Lord your God with all your heart, and with all your soul, and with all your strength, and with all your mind; and your neighbor as yourself" (10:27). Theologians tell us that there is a definite sense in which love of God and love of neighbor are one love, and for a married man his first "neighbor" is his wife.[4] A Catholic man needs to remember these words from the First Letter of John: "...those who do not love a brother or sister whom they have seen, cannot love God whom they have not seen" (4:20).

At the same time, it is important to reject the nonsense that loving my neighbor is the only way I can love God. Loving God directly, in prayer, is essential to a Christian life.

Fidelity to his marriage is central to a married man's faith and his relationship with Christ. He knows that there is nothing more important in this life than being faithful to his marriage, and temptations to and opportunities for sexual infidelity are not uncommon. At the same time, it is important for a man to understand that there are more ways than adultery to be "unfaithful" to his wife. Sexual infidelity is, in fact, far from the most common way in which men violate their marriage vows. A man can commit "adultery" with his career, business, or job. A man can even commit "adultery" with his golf game or sports programs on television. For a Catholic married man who takes his baptism seriously, marital fidelity means making his marriage the top priority in his life. His marriage deserves time and energy, just as his work gets his time and energy. If work comes between husband and wife for an extended period, then work may become a false god, and nothing will kill a marriage, or a faith, faster than idol worship. Sacrifices may need to be made for the sake of a marriage, and sometimes those sacrifices are professional or financial.

The flip side of this coin is the man who fails to hold up his end of the partnership. In an era when both spouses often must work, there are men who do not contribute their fair share to the family's income, who may not even bring home a regular paycheck. Such a man is the opposite of the workaholic husband. Perhaps he is too picky about the kind of work he is willing to do, so he does little or no income-producing work at all. This kind of man is sometimes the sort who also shows little enthusiasm for housework and childcare, so his wife ends up with double the burden, working both on the job and at home. The injustice of this situation is clear. Now we're talking about a genuinely unhealthy marriage and a genuinely unhealthy parenting situation. A "real man" thinks of himself as an equal partner in marriage and parenting. Any man who fails to shoulder his share of both economic and domestic burdens can hardly claim to be taking his faith seriously.

At the same time, it is also true that men's and women's approaches to marriage and family life are different and complementary. Women are, generally speaking, more naturally "gifted" when it comes to being married. For women, human intimacy comes more naturally. Men need to "work at" intimacy more consciously than women do, need to make a particular effort to gain "intimacy skills." These include communication skills, such as listening with empathy and becoming comfortable with self-revelation. When men have these skills, they can experience genuine intimacy, and they find it enormously rewarding.

It may come as a surprise to male Catholics, but when it

comes to listening and self-revelation, the Jesus of John's Gospel is an ideal model for married men. Jesus listens not just with his ears but with his heart, he readily reveals himself to others, and he allows others to reveal themselves to him. The fourth gospel's account of Jesus' encounter with two women, Mary and Martha, on the death of their brother, Lazarus, is a good example:

> When Martha heard that Jesus was coming, she went and met him, while Mary stayed at home. Martha said to Jesus, "Lord, if you had been here, my brother would not have died. But even now I know that God will give you whatever you ask of him." Jesus said to her, "Your brother will rise again." Martha said to him, "I know that he will rise again in the resurrection on the last day." Jesus said to her, "I am the resurrection and the life. Those who believe in me, even though they die, will live, and everyone who lives and believes in me will never die. Do you believe this?" She said to him, "Yes, Lord, I believe that you are the Messiah, the Son of God, the one coming into the world."
>
> When she had said this, she went back and called her sister Mary, and told her privately, "The Teacher is here and is calling for you." And when she heard it, she got up quickly and went to him. Now Jesus had not yet come to the village, but was still at the place where Martha had met him. The Jews who were with her in the house, consoling her, saw Mary get up quickly and go out. They followed her because they thought that she was going to the tomb to weep there. When Mary came where Jesus was and saw him, she knelt at his feet and said to him, "Lord, if you had been here, my brother would not have died."

When Jesus saw her weeping, and the Jews who came with her also weeping, he was greatly disturbed in spirit and deeply moved. He said, "Where have you laid him?" They said to him, "Lord, come and see." Jesus began to weep (11:20–35).

This story of the encounter between Jesus and the two grieving sisters, Mary and Martha, is one of the most powerful in the entire New Testament. More specifically, it is one of the most powerful examples of Jesus' relationships with women. Catholic married men will find in this account a Jesus who relates to women both as a good listener and as one who does not hesitate to reveal his inner self.

When Martha complains to Jesus, in effect taking him to task for not arriving sooner, Jesus does not become defensive. He does not say, "Hey, I was busy. I had important things to take care of. I got here as soon as I could." Instead, he invites Martha to a deeper faith, to deeper trust. Later, when Mary arrives, she voices the same complaint as Martha. If Jesus had been there, Lazarus would not have died. This time, Jesus' response is nonverbal. The narrator tells us only about Jesus' emotional reaction. He is "greatly disturbed in spirit and deeply moved."

Typically, we hear remarks on this passage that go something like this: "See what a good example Jesus sets for men. See how in touch he is with his feelings. Jesus feels the sorrow of those around him, and he empathizes." All this may be perfectly true, but notice what Jesus does next. In typical male fashion he does not dwell on his feelings or "get into" his emotions as an end in themselves. He does not simply listen and accept the feelings of those who are grieving. Rather, he immediately *does something* about his feelings and about the situation in which he finds himself. He wants to solve the problem—which is what men are inclined to do. He seeks information: "Where have you laid him?" Then he goes and does something about the source of the sadness: he brings Lazarus back to life.

The Jesus of this narrative in John's Gospel is both a "sensitive male" and a typical one. In Jesus we find the ideal balance of "sensitive guy" and problem-solver. He listens, he accepts the anguish of Martha and Mary, but he is not about to let it go at that. He wants to take action, and he does so. As most men are inclined to do, he wants to address the problem and do something about it in order to help Mary and Martha feel better again.

In the context of marriage and family life, this is the balance men should strive to attain, a balance of listening and accepting as well as trying to solve problems. Sometimes when a woman is emotionally distraught she says that all she wants her husband to do is listen and accept. She doesn't want her husband to try to do anything to help her feel better. Women need to understand, however, that this is not how men are put together. It's difficult for a man not to want to solve the problem. It may take extra effort on a woman's part to help her husband realize that the best way to "solve the problem" is *not* to try to solve the problem. Men, for their part, can come to understand this paradox and learn to live with it, but they will still feel compelled to "do something." Such inclinations do not go away just because a man has an intellectual grasp of the apparent contradictions of female psychology.

Another example of Jesus' male psychology—this time explicitly in the context of family relationships—is the account of the wedding at Cana, once again in John's Gospel:

...there was a wedding in Cana of Galilee, and the mother of Jesus was there. Jesus and his disciples had also been invited to the wedding. When the wine gave out, the mother of Jesus said to him, "They have no wine." And Jesus said to her, "Woman, what concern is that to you and to me? My hour has not yet come." His mother said to the servants, "Do whatever he tells you" (2:1–5).

Mary is the one who notices that "the wine gave out," not Jesus. He is completely oblivious. Then, when his mother points out the fact that the wine is all gone, Jesus replies in a typically male fashion: "So?" Jesus seems to have zero social skills, and his sensitivity leaves much to be desired.

We do not know what Jesus had been doing up to this point. Why did he not notice the lack of wine himself? Who knows? Maybe he was helping in the kitchen or with some other task. This would not be unlikely, given men's tendency to be task-oriented. Perhaps Jesus' focus was on the job at hand, while Mary was more in the "cast a wide net" mode, so she would become aware of the need for more wine before Jesus or most of the other men would have.

Furthermore, once Mary tells Jesus about the lack of wine, he seems uninterested in doing anything about it. It's not his job.

Mary knows Jesus can do something to help, however, and once she makes her wishes known, Jesus takes care of the problem. He seems to do this for his mother's sake, more than for the sake of the bride and groom.

This is the way men are, especially in the context of family relationships. They may sometimes seem uninspired, even insensitive by female standards. Even Jesus seems to be so in the story of the wedding at Cana. But, like Jesus, when push comes to shove, men are ready to do wonders for the sake of those they love.

When it comes to a man's role as husband and father, we may find particular inspiration in the example of Joseph, in the Gospel of Matthew. For many generations Saint Joseph was held up as an example for Catholic husbands and fathers, but there was something distinctly uninspiring about the way he was portrayed, as an old man who dedicated his life to preserving Mary's virginity. Granted, Joseph and Mary were not your typical married couple when it came to sex—that is not the theological point of either Mary's virginity or Joseph's celibacy. The theological point of both is to highlight the extraordinary identity of Jesus as the Son of God. Secondarily, the point is the total dedication of Mary and Joseph to doing God's will in all things. This same dedication, however, may exist just as much in the marriage of a typical, sexually active couple as in the exceptional marriage of Joseph and Mary. Virginity and celibacy are not the point; dedication to God is the point.

The Gospel of Matthew is different from Luke's Gospel in various ways, but the two gospels' infancy narratives are unique in the context of the present discussion. Matthew tells the story of Jesus' conception and birth from Joseph's perspective, whereas Luke's account is from Mary's point of view. So it is to Matthew that we will give our attention, to see what we may learn from Joseph about being a husband and father.

Matthew tells the story of Joseph's key role in the lives of Jesus and Mary in three parts. The first recounts the conception of Jesus by the Holy Spirit; the second tells of the visit by the Wise Men; and the third follows the little family as they flee by night into Egypt to escape the wrath of Herod. Here is the first part:

Now the birth of Jesus the Messiah took place in this way. When his mother Mary had been engaged to Joseph, but before they lived together, she was found to be with child from the Holy Spirit. Her husband Joseph, being a righteous man and unwilling to expose her to public disgrace, planned to dismiss her quietly. But just when he had resolved to do this, an angel of the Lord appeared to him in a dream and said, "Joseph, son of David, do not be afraid to take Mary as your wife, for the child conceived in her is from the Holy Spirit. She will bear a son, and you are to name him Jesus, for he will save his people from their sins." All this took place to fulfill what had been spoken by the Lord through the prophet:

"Look, the virgin shall conceive and bear a son,
and they shall name him Emmanuel,"

which means, "God is with us." When Joseph awoke from sleep, he did as the angel of the Lord commanded him; he took her as his wife, but had no marital relations with her until she had borne a son; and he named him Jesus (1:18–25).

The first thing we learn about Joseph is that he and Mary are engaged to be married, but immediately Joseph finds himself faced with a difficult decision. Mary is pregnant, and he knows that he is not the father. What should he do? In ancient Israel, if a young woman was found to be pregnant in such circumstances, the typical punishment was death by stoning. Joseph, "being a righteous man," wishes to spare Mary any such consequence, so he decides to "dismiss her quietly." He is willing to give her the benefit of the doubt, and it is precisely in this that he shows himself to be "a righteous man." Joseph refuses to condemn Mary, even though there can be no explanation for her pregnancy except sexual intercourse with another man.

Think about this. Put yourself in Joseph's place. Imagine being a young engaged man. Imagine discovering that your future spouse is pregnant by another man. You would feel deeply hurt, not to mention angry, indignant, outraged. According to the traditions of Israel, you would have every right to demand that Mary be condemned to death for adultery. You would have the right, in fact, to throw the first stone. But Joseph does not do this. He is prepared to forgive Mary, even though he can no longer marry her. Joseph's example of compassion stands as a model for all husbands for all time—as a challenge to every Christian husband who has ever been offended or hurt by his wife.

Before Joseph can carry out his plan to "dismiss her quietly," however, something astonishing happens. Joseph has a dream in which "an angel of the Lord" instructs him to go ahead and take Mary as his wife because the boy she is carrying is not just any child. The child "is from the Holy Spirit." Not only that, but this child has a special mission from God. So Joseph wakes up and is obedient to the angel's message.

Joseph was a dreamer, a visionary who was able to believe the angel in his dream. He was someone who could imagine the unimaginable and live his life accordingly. Joseph couldn't prove that his dream was not simply the product of an overactive nocturnal imagination. He just took it on faith and acted on faith, which is what a Catholic father is called to do, as well. Like Joseph, a Catholic father is called to be a man willing to live for his wife and family from a perspective radically conditioned by faith. Like Saint Joseph, a Catholic husband and father is called to be a risktaker.

The second part of Matthew's narrative is the account of the visit of the Wise Men with Herod; the visit of the Wise Men at the house in Bethlehem where Mary, Joseph, and Jesus are living; and the subsequent departure of the Wise Men. Joseph has no active role to play in this relatively brief interlude.

In the third part of the narrative, Matthew returns Joseph to his central role in the ongoing story:

> Now after they had left, an angel of the Lord appeared to Joseph in a dream and said, "Get up, take the child and his mother, and flee to Egypt, and remain there until I tell you; for Herod is about to search for the child, to destroy him." Then Joseph got up, took the child and his mother by night, and went to Egypt, and remained there until the death of Herod (2:13–15).

Once again, Matthew portrays Joseph as a dreamer and risk-taker. Based on information gathered in a dream, Joseph collects his little family and hotfoots it to a foreign country to live, for an indeterminate period, someplace he and Mary have never been before. Think of all they had to leave behind—the security of home and families, perhaps steady work, and who knows what else. For as long as they lived in Egypt, all they had was one another.

The third part of Matthew's narrative concludes:

> When Herod died, an angel of the Lord suddenly appeared in a dream to Joseph in Egypt and said, "Get up, take the child and his mother, and go to the land of Israel, for those who were seeking the child's life are dead." Then Joseph got up, took the child and his mother, and went to the land of Israel. But when he heard that Archelaus was ruling

over Judea in place of his father Herod, he was afraid to go there. And after being warned in a dream, he went away to the district of Galilee. There he made his home in a town called Nazareth... (2:19–23).

Joseph remains a dreamer, visionary, and man of faith. His faith in God determines his actions, and his main concern is doing what is best for his family. He does not ask, "Will I be able to find work as a carpenter in Egypt?" He goes, sight unseen, as soon as he knows that this is necessary for the safety of the child. His need to work to support his family will take care of itself, and apparently it did.

Whether this narrative is historical in the modern sense of the word is irrelevant for our purposes. The point is that Matthew's Gospel shows Joseph to be a man of deep faith and trust in God. Joseph is, in fact, a model of faith for husbands and fathers today.

The final observation this chapter will make is that Jesus clearly preferred the metaphor of "Father" (*Abba,* literally "loving Papa") to refer to God.[5] If there is any truth to the insights of modern psychology, we can only conclude that Jesus must have loved his earthly father, Joseph, a great deal. Otherwise, it would not have been so natural and easy for Jesus to call God his Father.

This may be surprising, since Jesus' mother, Mary, plays a much more prominent role in his life and in the subsequent life of the Church. Perhaps one reason Christians clung to Jesus' preference for calling God his Father, rather than introducing a Mother God, might be the desire to maintain Mary's special status as Mother of the Church. Perhaps the early Church called God our Father while at the same time encouraging devotion to Mary as *Theotokos,* the Mother of God and mother of all Christians.

We may say, then, that Catholic fathers are perfectly justified if they prefer to call God their Father, too. Men need a Father God to whom they can turn, upon whose help they can rely, whose love they can feel, and to whom they can respond in prayer. When fathers feel a deep love for their children, they can realize that the love they feel is but an echo of the love their Father in heaven feels for them. In other words, Catholic fathers can rely on their own experience to teach them about God who is their Father above all else.

With this observation in mind, we conclude this chapter with some words from Clayton C. Barbeau, who wrote an award-winning book for Catholic fathers many years ago:

> God has given the father of the family a share in the enriching of the universe by bringing into it more love. If God praises and rewards the faithful servant for the fruitful use of his five talents [see Matthew 25:15–28], what praise, what reward, will God reserve for the father who has cherished his wife and, with her, raised up for God the human lives entrusted to them, lives worth more than all the gold and silver in the world?[6]

Chapter 6
A Catholic Man's Approach to His Parish

A MAN'S PARISH is where his participation in the life of the Church takes on a wider dimension. Although the family, not the parish, is the most fundamental form of Church life, a man's parish membership is nevertheless indispensable to his Catholic identity and his ongoing experience of faith. A man can hardly call himself "a practicing Catholic" unless he identifies with and joins in the liturgical, educational, and social life of a local parish. Catholicism is communal, and no one can be a good Catholic in isolation. At the same time, Catholicism is by no means a jolly club one joins for merely social diversions. The purpose of a parish is not pious chumminess.

Paradoxically, for a man to be able to participate fully in the life of his parish, he needs to be secure in his solitude. We come into this world alone, and we go out of it alone. Solitude is the ultimate human condition, and anyone who ignores this fact or tries to escape it is bound to live an empty and inauthentic life. Only when a man finds God in solitude will his faith be that of a mature adult. The twentieth-century English philosopher Alfred North Whitehead spoke well when he said that religion is what one does with one's solitude.

Solitude and loneliness are not the same. A man can be lonely when he is surrounded by people, and anything but lonely when he is in solitude. In genuine solitude, a man discovers his true self, and only when this true self is actualized does a man become capable of entering into mutually beneficial relationships with others. "No one can safely go among men," says *The Imitation of Christ* (early fifteenth century), "but the man who loves solitude. No one can safely speak, but the man who loves silence" (I:xx).

In other words, parish community happens best when the community is made up of people who know who they are and what they believe in, people whose faith is both personal and communal. Drop one side of the equation and the other one fails as well. This is why it is so important for a parish to encourage prayerful solitude among the members of the parish as well as cultivating the community life of the parish itself. Having more of a natural inclination toward solitude—that is, being less inclined to group-based activities than women—men would not normally have a difficult time entering into prayerful solitude.

In his novel *Wobegon Boy,* humorist and sometime folk theologian Garrison Keillor offers an amusing but accurate description of the lives of the Norwegian bachelor farmers who live near his fictional town of Lake Wobegon, Minnesota. Garrison Keillor's words echo a dimension of common male experience:

> A bachelor farmer...wakes up in the morning and gets dressed in his old clothes and does a few chores, lets out the cat, pitches the empties from last night onto the pile

beside the garage, toasts him a couple frozen waffles and slathers them with butter and syrup and they're good, so he has two more, and all this time nobody has said to him, "Why don't you ever talk to me anymore?" He has a right to remain silent. That's his body rhythm. He puts on his barn jacket and goes out and works for a couple hours on projects for which there is no logical explanation, he sorts out coffee cans full of stuff, he shores up things, he pours some concrete, and then maybe he crawls back in the sack for a couple hours or he reads a book, and suddenly it's three in the afternoon. There is nothing special about three P.M., it is only a point on the clock, no law says you can't have lunch then. He opens a can of beans and eats a few off the top and shakes some ketchup on and horseradish and turns on the radio and the weather forecast is for more snow, which is fine with him. He puts mustard on a wiener and eats it. He feeds the cat and drives to town and parks the truck and goes into the Sidetrack Tap and gets a beer and a bump and now he may speak his first words of the day. Or he may not. It is up to him....He keeps a big dog around the place, who goes after strangers like a werewolf. He hasn't bathed today and maybe not yesterday. Why? Because he knows who he is....You can see that this guy is not operating on a strict schedule. Nobody is going to burn his butt if he doesn't get home by six o'clock.

The humor of this description of the life lived by a bachelor farmer is clear, of course, but Garrison Keillor's underlying point is a perfectly serious one. Virtually all men, no matter how happily married they may be, no matter how dedicated they are to their family, no matter how involved they are in their parish, have a streak of the bachelor farmer in them. Men like to have times when they can be alone and answerable to no one.

If a woman goes on a retreat at a monastery, say, where silent solitude is available in abundance, she will take advantage of that opportunity. But give her a chance to get together and talk with others at that monastery and she is unlikely to pass up the chance. A man, on the other hand, with few exceptions will prefer to dive into solitude, keep his mouth shut, and stay that way. Of course, there are male chatterboxes who couldn't stay alone in solitude for more than five minutes if their lives depended on it. But scratch the surface of such a man and chances are you will find the source of his compulsive verbosity to be something less than complete spiritual and emotional health.

Anyone, male or female, may be unable to deal with solitude for precisely the reason that he or she needs it. Solitude forces him or her to face up to God and self, and for some people this can be a terrifying prospect. A reasonably healthy, balanced male, however, is more likely than a reasonably healthy, balanced female to remain silent and solitary, given the opportunity. At the same time, a woman is more likely than a man to seek out conversational companions, in a retreat setting, for perfectly healthy, balanced motives.

It is important for parish leaders and parish ministries to be aware of this natural male inclination, especially when it is time to schedule parish retreats and the like. Instead of participating in retreats that include both men and women, Catholic men would most likely benefit more from all-male retreats. In decades gone by—specifically, during the pre-Vatican II decades of the 1940s, 1950s, and early 1960s—retreats for men and retreats for women were commonplace, and they were well attended, perhaps because they allowed spouses to have some time away from each other, a notion not included, in those days, in the prevalent understanding of a healthy marriage. Additionally, instead of coercing men into a lengthy schedule of "discussion groups," retreats for men need to allow time for solitary reflection and prayer. Solitude is a deep well from which a man can draw much spiritual nourishment, and he should not be made to feel that he is being a spiritual party pooper if he prefers solitude to group activities.

An effective men's retreat might take its inspiration from Scripture, allowing men to draw life from the Bible's heavily male character, from the maleness of Jesus, and from the predominance of masculine references for God. Such a retreat would address the real issues in the real lives of real Catholic men. At the same time, a Scripture-based retreat would inspire men, from a renewed sense of spiritual strength, to relate to their wives and to the other women in their lives from a position of equality and complementarity, as the Jesus of the gospels does, and not from a position of dominance. It is vital that retreats for men allow men to do more than simply react to issues raised by feminism.

Sometimes called "retreats," secular "men's movement" activities typically take their inspiration from a blend of folk myths and Jungian psychology. Sometimes they involve men gathering in a forest to sit around a campfire at night and beat on drums. Such experiences may have some value, but as far as Catholic men are concerned, they fall short of addressing what it means to live an explicitly Christian life in today's world. For Catholic men, the question of what it means to be a man cannot be separated from what it means to be a follower of Christ. A retreat for Catholic men would take this understanding for granted.

As would any educational opportunities a parish might provide for its men, including classes on masculine spirituality, discussion sessions for men on marriage and family-life issues, Bible study designed and directed by men themselves with men's questions and perspectives in mind, discussions of liturgical issues, lectures on spirituality and work...the possibilities are extensive. The important thing is that all sessions for men be designed with the assumption that a man's experience can be a source of revelation. God speaks to a man not only through Scripture, not only in the sacraments, not only by means of official Church teachings, but through his own personal male experience of life, relationships, the world, and the Church.

It may come as a surprise to men to hear that they can find God, the Divine Mystery, in their own male experience, but this is one of the most important messages a Catholic man can take from this book. Men have heard for decades that women need to find their own unique identity, that who they are does not depend on their husbands' identity, and so forth. Men need to hear the same messages. Who a man is does not depend on who the woman is that he is married to. Men have an identity independent of that of their wives. Men are not the work they do or the profession they are involved in; they are unique individuals with a unique identity, and God speaks in their everyday experience.

To tap into this source of spirituality, parish leaders would do well to schedule two or three "listening sessions" in which men are given the opportunity, first, to talk with one another in small groups. The questions posed to the group would be designed to discover men's needs in relation to being Catholic and being members of this particular parish. Each small group might then appoint a spokesman, and that man would report to the larger group on the list of needs, questions, complaints, and issues surfaced by his small group. At the end of such a session, parish leaders would have a list of Catholic men's needs to which the parish can respond in practical ways. The overall result would be a parish that is more "male friendly."

While a Catholic man appreciates the opportunities for spiritual growth he encounters through his parish, a man's parish is primarily where he hopes to receive support for his marriage and for his role as a father. Most parish leaders do not think of this assistance as a major priority for the parish. Consequently, many men have mixed feelings about their parishes. They want to participate in the life of the Church, but they rarely get the support they need from their parish, so they find it difficult to get enthusiastic when the collection basket comes around or a call goes out for volunteers. Even more so after having listened to a homily that is a well-meant exercise in pious verbosity. The sermon is one of the most important occasions for having an impact on the faith of men in the parish—for helping them deal with their day-to-day concerns about being a good Catholic husband and father. Unfortunately, most homilies commit the serious offense of making religion sound boring to men—this in spite of the fact that the homilist most often is male.[1]

Parishes that want to reach men will make a concerted effort to address homilies to men and/or women, rather than delivering homilies that ignore gender or appeal to some androgynous orientation. There are no androgynes sitting in the pews, only men and women. If homilies are to have an impact, they need to touch the real experiences of real men and real women. Men—to stick to the topic of this book—are most likely to respond to a homily that reflects an awareness of their experiences. This means that the homilist regularly needs to spend time with laymen and not limit his male friendships to other priests. He needs to take seriously novelist Ron Hansen's remarks (see page VII) about the real issues in men's lives today. Otherwise, how can he expect to speak to the experiences of Catholic men?

Catholic men also search for relevance in the weekly liturgy, but more and more the Church's liturgy seems irrelevant to its men. While women may find masculine metaphors and pronouns for God offensive, men find them energizing. To men, addressing God as Father is a way of receiving God's self-gift, of receiving grace. As suggested in chapter 3, feminists of both sexes who remove all masculine metaphors and pronouns for God from liturgical texts, often substituting the impersonal term "God," need to understand that addressing an impersonal deity instead of a personal one is no great advance. It is possible to modify traditional formulas in ways that are beneficial for both men and women.

Take one example. The traditional trinitarian formula speaks, "In the name of the Father, and of the Son, and of the Holy Spirit." One well-meaning modification of the traditional formula goes like this: "In the name of the one God and Mother of us all, Father, Son, and Holy Spirit." This scrambled concoction makes no theological sense. How can "one God" be "Mother of us all" as well as "Father, Son, and Holy Spirit"?

In one of his novels Father Andrew M. Greeley suggests a gentler, more poetic, and more theologically responsible modification.[2] Father Greeley's main character, Bishop Blackie Ryan, administers the sacrament of confirmation "in the name of the Father, and of the Son, and of the Holy Spirit Herself." The addition of a single feminine pronoun smoothly adds a feminine dimension to the trinitarian formula while leaving the traditional images intact, and this addition requires no mental contortions to grasp its meaning. Father Greeley's approach allows a healthy development in our understanding, whereas the former approach goes after the traditional formula with a verbal wrecking ball.

Father Greeley often uses strong, playful feminine images

of God, but he also uses feminine images of God that appeal to heterosexual men. Retaining the scriptural perspective, he seems to take seriously the relatively few scriptural images of God that are feminine: for example, the highly erotic feminine images in the Song of Songs—divinely inspired, as is all of Scripture. Why not use feminine images of God as lover, images that will appeal specifically to men, instead of using impersonal action-titles such as "birthing God"?

Trying to make liturgical language meaningful for men in ways that will not offend anyone may, however, be next to impossible. So sensitive are many Catholics to issues of language that no matter what anyone does, someone is likely to object. For years to come this may remain a no-win situation.

In addition to the feminization of liturgical language, many parishes are feminized in so many other ways—in spite of what Catholic feminists may think, and in spite of the sometimes legitimate complaints they may level at certain conventional Church practices—that many men feel uncomfortable being there at all. From liturgies to educational programs, the emphasis on "sharing feelings," holding hands, and speaking of God in feminine terms leaves many men feeling unwelcome at best. One Catholic woman hit the bull's-eye in the Catholic biweekly magazine *Commonweal*. She responded to a question about women's ordination by saying, "We already run the Church."[3] On the parish level, and sometimes on the diocesan level, this woman couldn't be more accurate. While feminine influences are needed as a corrective to past imbalances, such imbalances are no justification for overlooking the equally significant needs of Catholic men.

Nevertheless, Catholic men, like many Catholic women, will continue to participate in Sunday celebrations of the Eucharist even when they do not show up for anything else. Sometimes parish staff are inclined to be critical of men who only attend Mass but rarely appear for parish social or educational events. While this is understandable, it may also reveal a certain narrow perspective. Those critics may do well to recall that there is more than one acceptable way to understand the Church—that is, there is more than one valid ecclesiology.

Sometimes people who are professional Church ministers, whether lay or clergy, think and operate out of a single dominant "model of the Church," to recall a term made popular by theologian Father Avery Dulles, S.J., in *Models of the Church*.[4] Parishes are urban and suburban and rural, small and large, conservative and progressive and middle-of-the-road, ethnic and ethnically mixed. Some are impossible to categorize. Still, all parishes tend to be similar in terms of their structures, ministries, and programs. Furthermore, the model of the Church out of which most parish ministers operate today—particularly in progressive parishes—is a communal one, an understanding of the Church that places a great deal of emphasis on togetherness and social interaction. According to this perspective, it is essential for Catholics to give considerable time to parish social, educational, and service-oriented activities. Anyone who largely limits his or her participation in parish life to liturgical gatherings falls short of the ideal, is not a "good" Catholic.

In a second edition of his book, published twenty-three years after the first edition, Father Dulles added a new chapter titled "The Church: Community of Disciples," which articulates an excellent understanding of the communal model while avoiding the notion that this is the *only* acceptable model of the Church. Father Dulles clarifies the vital connections between active Christian discipleship, for example, and the parish as a community. At the same time, he insists that no single model of the Church is the only valid one. "The Church, as a mystery, transcends all creaturely analogies and defies reduction to a single theological paradigm."⁵

For the sake of the Catholic men in their parishes, pastors and parish ministers would do well to temper their disapproval of men who are not heavily involved in "building the parish community." They can do this, as indicated earlier, with a look at how "male friendly" the parish truly is, and just as important, with a commitment to a more balanced ecclesiology, one that allows for more than one rather narrowly understood model of the Church. To borrow again from Father Dulles, "the Church as Institution," "the Church as Sacrament," and "the Church as Mystical Communion" all allow for less emphasis on communal togetherness than many progressive parish ministers hold as the ideal. Yet they are all perfectly valid understandings of the Church. They allow men to sidestep attempts to "lay guilt trips" on them for making participation in Sunday Mass their main form of participation in the life of their parish.

Some Catholic men become alienated from the Church due to other unpleasant experiences they have had with their parishes. Even if they continue attending Sunday Mass, they keep their distance because they view the parish as an institution with its shoelaces tied together. Not only do they rarely receive from their parish the support they need for marriage and family life. Not only do they rarely, if ever, hear men's critical life issues addressed in homilies. Frequently, men discover that they are treated as something less than the responsible, experienced, knowledgeable adults that they are. A Catholic businessman, for example, may be asked to head up his parish's finance committee, only to discover that his suggestions for managing the parish's financial resources are ignored in the end because the pastor does whatever he wants to anyway. Such a response hardly encourages volunteerism among men.

But Catholic men need to resist being "typecast" in their parishes anyway. Instead of merely trying to apply their professional or vocational skills in the context of parish life, they would do well to extend themselves into areas where, initially, they may not feel particularly qualified. Instead of volunteering to be on the finance committee, a businessman could offer to join the liturgy committee. Liturgy committees need the perspectives of men who try to live their faith every day in the knockabout world as well as in the context of marriage and family life.

Indeed, there is no dimension of parish life that would not benefit from the faith, experience, and insights of men. When female perspectives dominate parishes, the result is unbalanced parishes. Granted, we live in an era heavily influenced by women and women's concerns. But should men allow their needs and insights to be dismissed as "hopelessly patriarchal" before they even get a chance to speak for themselves? Sometimes Catholic men fail to realize that their needs and perspectives are valid, too, and deserve respect and attention. A Catholic man should not apologize for being male.

In our time, many Catholic men secretly feel that they should. Angry Catholic feminists, women and men, object to any maleness in the Church. They object to the historically conditioned masculine language of Scripture and liturgy and to a males-only priesthood. Whether their objections are justified or not is debatable, but in the face of unspoken feminist "infallibility" and, sometimes, self-righteous rage, many men feel powerless to do anything but shut up, go along, and silently apologize for being male.

Catholic feminists may accuse men of grabbing all the power in the Church, but most ordinary Catholic men have no more power than women have. Certainly they have no more power to change Church structures than do women. The typical male Catholic is as much in need of spiritual empowerment as his female counterpart, and this is where parish leaders can do some good. They can strive to empower men as much as they strive to empower women. They can address men's issues in homilies as often as they address women's issues. They can strive for language in liturgical texts that is faithful to both Scripture, sacred tradition, and contemporary experience. They can listen to Catholic men and respond to their spiritual, religious, and human needs in ways men will find helpful. If all of this happens, Catholic men will return to active participation in their parishes in numbers many parish ministers will find astonishing.

Chapter 7

A Catholic Man Follows Christ in the Church

AS WE NOTED in earlier chapters, central to a Catholic man's faith is his ongoing intimacy with the risen Christ. He looks to the man Jesus in the gospels for guidance and inspiration. The fact that the Jesus of the gospels is male, and the fact that the gospels were written by men—albeit drawing on the faith experience of both men and women—is significant for men in the Church, for their spirituality and understanding of themselves as disciples of Christ.

Once again, to point this out is not an attempt to undermine the concerns of women in the Church. What women do about the fact of Jesus' maleness is not the concern of this book. Rather, to focus on Jesus' masculinity is simply to take advantage of a historical, human, and theological fact as a source of understanding and inspiration for men today. Regardless of any benefits that may accrue to men, directly or indirectly, as a result of efforts to advance the cause of women in the Church, men need not apologize for asking, for their own well-being, about the meaning of Jesus' maleness. In the long run, the answer to this question will benefit women as well as men because it is to women's advantage, too, for men to be healthier, stronger, and more balanced in every aspect of their existence.

The particular focus of this chapter, then, is on how men may follow Christ specifically in the context of the Church. The underlying conviction here is that neither men nor women, as Catholics, can think of themselves in isolation from the entire Church. The first question we must ask—because, to quote the old hymn, "the Church's one foundation is Jesus Christ her Lord"—is: What can men learn from the Jesus of the gospels about their identity and vocation as Catholic men in the Church? One way to structure our response to this question is to do so chronologically, following a man from single young adulthood through to old age, examining specific related issues as we go.

Looking to Jesus for insight and inspiration has a unique value for a young, unmarried man, for the Jesus of the gospels is himself a young, unmarried man. Frequently, we overlook the significance of this fact. All four gospels take for granted that Jesus is an unmarried man in his mid- to late twenties. Pious religious art tends to portray Jesus as older than he was, as if he were in his mid-thirties, typically. But to do this is misleading. According to the traditional view, Jesus barely saw his thirties before he died.

Here is Jesus, a young man, and his religious mission is central to who he is and what he is about. From this fact young Catholic men can take encouragement for their own faith and active participation in the life of the Church. Following in Jesus' footsteps leaves no room for the common cultural assumption that there is something less than masculine about taking one's religion to heart.

In Mark's Gospel, the first words the young man Jesus speaks are these: "The time is fulfilled, and the kingdom of God has come near; repent, and believe in the good news" (1:15). Scripture scholars tell us that these words constitute the very heart of Jesus' message—his announcement that a historical moment of completion has arrived, an intersection of time and eternity we might say, so that God's personal presence in all of creation is somehow, mysteriously, closer than it was before. Because it is precisely in Jesus himself that God has come closer. So Jesus calls for "repentance," which means conversion, a radical turning around of one's whole being, a reorientation from self-centeredness toward other-centeredness, toward God and neighbor. The reason we can do this, Jesus says, is because we can accept unconditionally the "good news" that God loves us passionately, unconditionally, as a loving Papa loves his children.

This is the core of the Christian life, upon which everything else depends. In Mark's Gospel the young man Jesus speaks words that articulate an idealism to which any young Catholic man can give himself with all his heart. An idealism, based on faith, that can undergird any practical direction a young man's life may take. Pursuing an education, moving into the world of work, deciding whether to marry and whom to marry—all such concerns can draw life and meaning from the more fundamental dedication to following Christ and responding to his invitation to "repent, and believe in the good news."

The young man who dedicates himself to Christ, and who finds his fundamental self-understanding as a Catholic, will discover that his search for direction and purpose in life gains a focus and consistency that someone with no faith commitment will not have. This is not to say that a young man who embraces faith in Christ, within the living tradition and institutions of Catholicism, will not experience times of darkness, confusion, or difficulty. It simply means that even these periods will have meaning when understood in the context of a life given direction by faith.

Jesus' idealism, as we find it in the gospels, particularly Mark's, is the idealism of a young man. As you read the following words, keep in mind that the Jesus who speaks is young, perhaps twenty-eight years old:

> "No one sews a piece of unshrunk cloth on an old cloak; otherwise, the patch pulls away from it, the new from the old, and a worse tear is made. And no one puts new wine into old wineskins; otherwise, the wine will burst the skins, and the wine is lost, and so are the skins; but one puts new wine into fresh wineskins."
>
> One sabbath he was going through the grainfields; and as they made their way his disciples began to pluck heads of grain. The Pharisees said to him, "Look, why are they doing what is not lawful on the sabbath?" And he said to them, "Have you never read what David did when he and his companions were hungry and in need of food? He entered the house of God, when Abiathar was high priest, and ate the bread of the Presence, which it is not lawful for any but the priests to eat, and he gave some to his companions." Then he said to them, "The sabbath was made for humankind, and not humankind for the sabbath; so the Son of Man is lord even of the sabbath" (2:21–28).

Notice in the first two verses the contrast Mark's Jesus makes between the old and the new. Jesus insists that the new is superior to the old, a perspective characteristic of youthful idealism. Out with the old, in with the new.

In the following section, Jesus insists that religious laws and traditions are meant to serve people; traditions and laws are not an end in themselves. Again, this reflects the idealistic perspective of a young man, and his example is a good one for young Catholic men who may sometimes find it necessary to cope with religious institutions that have grown old, institutions that sometimes find it difficult to take seriously the ideals of the young man Jesus. Indeed, it may be the special role of young Catholic men to remind the Church of Jesus' idealism.

Older people frequently think that the young have everything to live for and should be filled with idealism, optimism, and hope. Sometimes, however, the opposite is true. Sometimes the young are the ones who need encouragement not to give up hope. G. K. Chesterton wrote:

> ...youth is the period in which a man can be hopeless. The end of every episode is the end of the world. But the power of hoping through everything, the knowledge that the soul survives its adventures, that great inspiration comes to the middle-aged; God has kept that good wine until now. It is from the backs of the elderly gentlemen that the wings of the butterfly should burst.[1]

Young Catholic men sometimes look around and wonder if the Church, the oldest institution in the Western world, can possibly survive when sometimes its leaders seem to want to live in the past. Young Catholic men sometimes witness the words and actions of Jesus in the gospels, then observe the words and actions of Church leaders, and they don't know what to make of the contrast. How can Church leaders sometimes be so out of synch with Jesus—with his idealism, his readiness to sacrifice everything for the truth, his obviously simple lifestyle, and his lack of concern for financial forms of security?

Young Catholic men need to listen not only to the idealism of Jesus in the gospels, however, but to how balanced he is. Jesus does not simply prefer the new to the old: he wants them both. In Matthew's Gospel, Jesus declares that those who have been "trained for the kingdom of heaven" are like "the master of a household who brings out of his treasure what is new and what is old" (13:52). Also, for all his negative comments about the Mosaic Law, Jesus also insists that the Law is not to be done away with; rather, it is superficial observance of the Law that he opposes. "Do not think that I have come to abolish the law or the prophets; I have come not to abolish but to fulfill. For truly I tell you, until heaven and earth pass away, not one letter, not one stroke of a letter, will pass from the law until all is accomplished" (5:17–18).

Jesus' revolution is one far more radical than any young/old, liberal/conservative distinction may suggest. Rather, he calls us to the heart of the matter, to living for God and neighbor as our top priority so that everything, old and new, serves this purpose. As a young man, Jesus stands as a model for young men who would embrace a wisdom far older and much newer than the frequently superficial "wisdom" of the present age. His idealism translates into a vision that embraces the present and the future while retaining the wisdom and traditions of the past. It is out of this broad, rich perspective that today's young men can construct the future of the Church.

During their twenties most young Catholic men seek to identify and pursue a specific vocation and profession, trade, or other form of work. By "vocation" we mean fundamental options such as marriage, religious life, priesthood, or singleness. From a Catholic faith perspective, the search for one's vocation, or calling from God, is clearly a religious one, a spiritual quest. In a culture that considers such concerns incidental or irrelevant, the young man who is prayerful about his quest for a vocation may find himself considered "weird" indeed. Yet following in the footsteps of the young man Jesus, and being open to the presence of the risen Christ here and now, is what a young Catholic man is called to. When a young man follows this path to the choice of a vocation, ultimately he will discover his own deepest self and his most fulfilling life project.

When it comes to seeking the work he will do, a young Catholic man will approach this project in a prayerful manner as well. It would be a mistake, however, to think of these matters as "spiritual problem solving." To seek God's will for me does not mean that I try to figure out what God wants me to do, as if he is keeping it a secret and I must try to talk him into revealing the secret to me so I'll know what to do with my life. On the contrary, two wills are involved, mine and God's, and both are free. I discover God's will for me by following and developing my natural talents and inclinations, and by using the other gifts God gives me. When it comes to work, in fact, I may do several kinds in the course of my lifetime, and all may be consistent with God's will for me. Also, God works with a man's free choices and brings to good even the mistakes or less-than-ideal choices he makes along the way.

For a Catholic man, when it comes to work, the important thing to keep in mind is that the work I do is a way to express love for God and neighbor. In virtually any kind of work, whether I enjoy it or find that I must simply do the job for the sake of my family, I can still do what I do as a follower of Christ—honestly, reliably, and in a spirit of service. Even being involuntarily unemployed can be a calling in the sense that it is an opportunity to grow in faith and trust.

The next stage of life for Catholic men is the one psychologists sometimes call the stage of generativity. For most men, this is the stage that includes the choice of a marriage partner, the ongoing project of being married, and two or three decades of parenting. For some men, the choice ends up being single life, while a few follow the alternate "track" of priesthood and/or life in a religious order or congregation.

As we discussed in chapter 5, if a Catholic man is married, his marriage is not peripheral or incidental to his faith; rather, it is at the very heart of what it means for him to be a Catholic follower of Christ. The first "neighbor" a married man is called to love is his wife. Thus being a good Catholic and a faithful husband go hand-in-hand, and the practical implications are not difficult to discover.

In the context of our discussion, it is important to point out that a Catholic man's marriage is also basic to his place in the Church. Indeed, for a married Catholic man, being a good Catholic cannot be separated from being a loving and faithful husband. Clearly understanding his relationship with the Church prior to and early in his marriage is particularly important for a married Catholic man. This is so because the potential for missing out on all that the Church could do to support and nourish a marriage is so great, and the threat to a marriage from the dominant secular culture is so real.

This being the case, one cannot help asking why there is so little support for married men in the Church. As an institution, the Church's record of support for marriage, and for married men in particular, is nothing to brag about. The Church is there for "the poor" through its charitable activities, and rightly so. The Church has countless liturgical, catechetical, social, and other ministries. Its support for marriage, however, is all but limited to programs for engaged couples. Were it not for Marriage Encounter weekends, for which the Church-as-institution can take no credit, Catholic marriages would receive virtually no support in a faith-based context. Rarely do priests—even permanent deacons, who typically are married themselves—preach on the goodness, value, and importance of marriage. Even more rarely do they preach on the goodness, value, and importance of being a husband and father in the Church.

During the "generative" years, most Catholic men become fathers. This role is vitally important to them and to anyone who would understand a Catholic man's spirituality during these years. Being a father is a tremendously rewarding and challenging vocation in our time, as in all times, yet once again the Church leaves fathers largely to their own devices, offering little, if any, help to Catholic fathers who would gain a deeper understanding of their role as fathers and of a supporting spirituality.

As noted in chapter 6, Catholic men, and fathers in particular, may feel devalued by the feminization of many parishes and of Catholicism in general—in everything from liturgy to catechetical programs, from parish ministries to Catholic publishing (which issues a steady stream of books on women's topics). Men recognize that it is currently politically risky in the American Church to focus on the fact that Jesus preferred to call God his *Abba*, "Father" or "loving Papa." Almost never do Catholic fathers hear homilies or catechetical lectures on what it means, theologically and/or spiritually, to call God our "Father." In none of the gospels does Jesus ever call God his "Mother." To point this out is, however, to assure oneself of being labeled a misogynist.

In chapter 3 we quoted from one of the very few books—it may be the only one—issued by a Catholic publisher in recent decades that argues for the importance of calling God "Father." John W. Miller is a Protestant Scripture scholar, and this may explain his willingness to publish such a book. At any rate, in

Biblical Faith and Fathering: Why We Call God "Father" Professor Miller explains why it is important for both men and women that we call God our Father, as Jesus did. The biological tie between father and children is far more tenuous than that which exists between mother and children. This is one major reason why God came to be understood using male metaphors, to help build a culture in ancient Israel in which fathers would act with love and faithfulness toward their spouse and children.

The fragile nature of the father-child bond is not as great as it once was. But it remains a fact today, as the many fatherless families in our society will attest. "To summarize," writes Professor Miller, "in that a child grows in the body of its mother, mothering is a biologically determined experience to a far greater extent than is fathering. By contrast, fathering is a predominantly cultural acquisition."[2] Our culture needs a God who is loving Father every bit as much as any earlier culture did.

The social sciences heavily document the importance of fathers in the lives of their children, and Catholic fathers carry a major responsibility when it comes to raising children. Catholic fathers need to understand the importance of what they are about. Yet the role of the father gets little more than lip service in the Church. As long as the metaphor Jesus preferred for God—namely, "Father"—is devalued by being cast in a politically incorrect light, Catholic fathers will experience that much less support for who they are and what they do.

A Catholic man whose vocation is marriage and parenting faces many personal issues related to his Catholic identity and Church membership that other men can address only from a distance. The best contemporary example is the Church's official prohibition of artificial contraception. A Catholic married man who takes his faith to heart will need to decide how he will relate to this official teaching. Among Catholics today there are essentially three paths. We will call these the traditionalist path, the enculturated path, and the moderate path.

Traditionalist Catholics insist that, in practice, artificial contraceptives may not be used because the official teaching of the Church says so. Conscience is free, but conscience is obligated to form itself according to the official teaching of the Church—which seems to mean that, in fact, conscience is not truly free to act contrary to the official teaching. This, in turn, seems to mean that there is no actual freedom of conscience. Traditionalist Catholics, while sincere in their adherence to the teachings of the Church, seem to suggest that there is no possibility of a distinction between the will of God and official Church teachings. As far as they are concerned, official Church teachings can never be in error, out of focus, or even a little bit mistaken.

Enculturated Catholics, at the other extreme, believe that one has no obligation to pay any attention at all to official Church teachings on anything having to do with human sexuality or social issues—indeed, any matter that touches their lives directly—because, they believe, such official teachings are automatically out of touch with reality. Enculturated Catholics are frequently nominal Catholics, rarely participating in the life of a parish or in the Eucharist. They live their lives primarily according to the values and ideals of the dominant secular culture, with little or no concern for the values of the gospel or of Catholicism. Hence, if they pay any attention to the official prohibition of artificial contraception, they reject it with no attempt to understand its rationale or consider its source.

Moderate Catholics take their faith seriously, respect the official teachings of the Church, but do not believe that all official Church teachings are infallible; neither do they believe that such teachings may be allowed to replace personal conscience.

Rather, the Church's official teachings on issues of sexual behavior, social issues, and so forth are meant to educate and inform conscience while leaving conscience free. Thus on the issue of artificial contraception, moderate Catholics study the official teaching carefully, make every attempt to understand its rationale, and prayerfully listen to both experts and ordinary people who praise or criticize this teaching.

In the end, moderate Catholics often find that they cannot accept the teaching of the Church that prohibits the use of artificial contraceptives. Yet they do not allow this position to alienate them from the Church or from living a Catholic life, receiving the sacraments, and so on. The difference between moderate and enculturated Catholics is that the former take the values of their faith tradition to heart and dissent from the official teaching with regret, all the while remaining open to further insights. The latter, on the other hand, remain largely indifferent to input from the gospel or Catholic teachings and traditions.

A Catholic married man would be well advised to follow the moderate path, taking his faith and the teachings of the Church to heart, but realizing that he must act always in freedom and according to the dictates of his conscience. This is so even in the relatively rare instance when conscience finds itself at odds with official Church teachings. In the final analysis, the moderate Catholic takes seriously these words from the *Catechism of the Catholic Church*:

> Man has the right to act in conscience and in freedom so as personally to make moral decisions. "He must not be forced to act contrary to his conscience. Nor must he be prevented from acting according to his conscience, especially in religious matters" (No. 1782).

This item from the *Catechism*, with its quotation from *Dignitates humanae* (no. 3), the Vatican II declaration on religious liberty, is a concise statement of the Church's "bottom line" on moral decision making. The *Catechism* includes statements about the importance of taking official Church teachings to heart, and about the relationship between personal conscience and official Church teachings, but the words quoted here constitute Catholicism's version of "the buck stops here."

Here is what all this adds up to: A Catholic married man needs to understand how important it is for him to make the effort to be well informed about the nature and purpose of official Church teachings, particularly in the context of his marriage. The secular media may give the impression that a "good Catholic" blindly obeys all official Church teachings, including the official prohibition of contraception. Vocal traditionalist Catholics will loudly proclaim a similar message. But such a simplistic understanding of what it means to be a Catholic is unworthy of a mature adult faith.

Regardless of the decision a Catholic married man ultimately makes, he must put in the effort to become well informed, to have a well-formed conscience. Then, when husband and wife together arrive at a decision, the decision is theirs alone, and they are responsible for it and its consequences. (Clearly, we are light years beyond the era when a husband would leave all matters concerning the spacing and limiting of children entirely up to his wife and her physician.) Whether the consequences are those expected or turn out to be a surprise, pleasant or unpleasant, husband and wife are responsible—not the Church, not theologians, and not "society." If husband and wife decide that, in good conscience, they must accept any and all children born to them, they cannot blame "the Church" for any consequences they may find unpleasant a few years down the line.

The final stage in a man's life is, of course, old age. Men who grow old in the Church today receive little, if any, attention and honor. They are as forgotten by their Church as they are by secular society and culture. Yet old age, like every other stage of life, is an experience of the Divine Mystery, a source of grace, and even a coming face-to-face with divine revelation in everyday experience. As a general rule, however, old men who are Catholics never hear such ideas from their Church, so they can only conclude that being old, they are of little value, even to their Church.

The older a Catholic man grows—and aging is meant to be a genuine form of *growth,* a sacramental experience, not mere deterioration—the more he discovers that the meaning of life is found not in accomplishments but in relationships. This is what the Church has told him all his life, and now he finds it to be true.

A Catholic man who is a grandfather knows what it means to be connected, to be at the leading edge of two younger generations. A grandfather is a man who has accomplished one mission, the raising of children to adulthood. Now, to his surprise and delight, he becomes a grandfather and once again a baby fills his arms, a young child climbs into his lap to have a story read, and his heart is full. Perhaps he reads to his grandchild the same stories he read to his own children when they were little. Perhaps as he does this his eyes fill with tears. Perhaps he knows a joy too deep for words.

Out of this experience of growing older and becoming a grandfather comes experiences that are sacred, experiences that teach the older Catholic man about God—can it be? oh, delightful!—who is not just a Father, a loving Papa, but yes, a Grandfather, too! God is a wonderful, surprising grandfather whose love for us is, at least remotely, like the love a human grandfather feels for his grandchildren. More and more a man learns about God from his own experience, even as a grandfather, from his love for his children's children.

Sometimes in our era grandfathers do not get to see their grandchildren as often as they would like, grandfathers and grandchildren living distant from one another. Sometimes being a grandfather is not a stress-free experience by any means. Sometimes a man becomes a grandfather when he would rather not, when a young adult offspring makes irresponsible choices and becomes a parent in circumstances that are not the best for all concerned. Still, there is this new life, and still, a man has become a grandfather, and he must choose to do this or choose to do that. What will it be? A Catholic man's heart will tell him, will teach him, if he listens closely. Through his intimacy with the risen Christ, the word of God will come to him if he listens in the quiet of his heart. He will be the grandfather he is called by his Father-God to be, even in circumstances that are not, it would seem, the best for all concerned.

Old age is, for a Catholic man, ultimately a time to let go. Slowly, gradually, as the times reveal it is time, the task is to look forward while still maintaining a focus on and a dedication to this time, this world, and the people who still need a man's love. It is a time to look forward to the Great Transition, to the flash of darkness called death that leads, instantly, to the final mystery, the great light we call, for lack of a better term, eternal life.

This dual focus in an old man's Catholic heart is the source of his greatest freedom and deepest capacity to give and receive love. An old man discovers that, after all the life he has lived, finally he knows the secret of what it means to truly be a man. In old age he discovers the secret of eternal youth because all his life he has been the closest of companions with the young man Jesus, the risen Christ. Looking back, everywhere he turns he sees that in all things and all places the closest of his friends has been the man Jesus, risen and alive always and everywhere. And this is enough, always and everywhere, for a Catholic man, always and everywhere enough.

Chapter 8

Catholic Men and Catholic Women

A ONE-LINER with a sharp edge circulated in a "stage whisper" among the men at an informal gathering of Catholic men and women academics. The one-liner went like this: "If a man says something when no women are present, is he still wrong?"

That such a one-liner should surface at all, much less in a gathering of Catholic academics, virtually all of whom have liberal theological credentials in good order, suggests that all is not well among Catholic men and women. And that Catholic men sometimes harbor resentment against women just as women do against men. As we've discussed possible sources of this resentment in previous chapters, this chapter will focus on what resources can help Catholic men who struggle with male/female issues, in the Church at large as well as in marriage and family life.

Men who wonder how to act in a manner consistent with their faith, in their relationships with women and with regard to women's issues in the Church and in society, do well to turn to the Jesus of the gospels for guidance and inspiration. For in him we find a man who transcended his culture's patriarchal attitudes toward women and addressed women on a basis of equal dignity. As portrayed in the gospels, Jesus suggests by word and action that men and women have more in common than not. To be more precise, as theologian Father Richard McBrien explains, in the gospels, Jesus' main concern is for "the *dignity of women,* which went far beyond contemporary Jewish attitudes and customs."[1]

At the same time, Jesus does not deny that men and women have their complementary differences, both physiological and emotional. In John's Gospel, for example, which reflects deep convictions about the dignity of women, Jesus uses a uniquely female example to make a point about discipleship because it suits his purposes best: "When a woman is in labor, she has pain, because her hour has come. But when her child is born, she no longer remembers the anguish because of the joy of having brought a human being into the world" (16:21). Jesus is no champion of androgyny. An experience unique to women suits his purpose, so he uses it—and in using it makes a counter-cultural statement, too.

To proclaim the kingdom of God, the Jesus of the gospels often ignored the cultural models of his time. John's Gospel provides one of the most dramatic examples:

> So he came to a Samaritan city called Sychar, near the plot of ground that Jacob had given to his son Joseph. Jacob's well was there, and Jesus, tired out by his journey, was sitting by the well. It was about noon.
>
> A Samaritan woman came to draw water, and Jesus said to her, "Give me a drink." (His disciples had gone to the city to buy food.) The Samaritan woman said to him, "How

is it that you, a Jew, ask a drink of me, a woman of Samaria?" (Jews do not share things in common with Samaritans.) Jesus answered her, "If you knew the gift of God, and who it is that is saying to you, 'Give me a drink,' you would have asked him, and he would have given you living water." The woman said to him, "Sir, you have no bucket, and the well is deep. Where do you get that living water? Are you greater than our ancestor Jacob, who gave us the well, and with his sons and his flocks drank from it?" Jesus said to her, "Everyone who drinks of this water will be thirsty again, but those who drink of the water that I will give them will never be thirsty. The water that I will give will become in them a spring of water gushing up to eternal life." The woman said to him, "Sir, give me this water, so that I may never be thirsty or have to keep coming here to draw water."

Jesus said to her, "Go, call your husband, and come back." The woman answered him, "I have no husband." Jesus said to her, "You are right in saying, 'I have no husband'; for you have had five husbands, and the one you have now is not your husband. What you have said is true!" The woman said to him, "Sir, I see that you are a prophet. Our ancestors worshiped on this mountain, but you say that the place where people must worship is in Jerusalem." Jesus said to her, "Woman, believe me, the hour is coming when you will worship the Father neither on this mountain nor in Jerusalem. You worship what you do not know; we worship what we know, for salvation is from the Jews. But the hour is coming, and is now here, when the true worshipers will worship the Father in spirit and truth, for the Father seeks such as these to worship him. God is spirit, and those who worship him must worship in spirit and truth." The woman said to him, "I know that Messiah is coming" (who is called Christ). "When he comes, he will proclaim all things to us." Jesus said to her, "I am he, the one who is speaking to you."

Just then his disciples came. They were astonished that he was speaking with a woman, but no one said, "What do you want?" or, "Why are you speaking with her?" (4:5-27).

The key moment comes at the end of this passage, where the words of Jesus' disciples clearly reflect the common prejudice against women. It is most revealing to read the last paragraph in this quotation, then go back and read from the beginning. All the way through, notice the recurring phrases "Jesus said to her" and "The woman said to him." The dialogue John gives us is a conversation between *equals*. There is no indication whatsoever that Jesus thinks of the Samaritan woman as inferior to himself, a man. Had the person Jesus encountered in this situation been a man, Jesus would have spoken to him in the same way he speaks to the woman.

In fact, as far as the narrator in John's Gospel is concerned, it is more significant that the woman is a Samaritan—thus alienated from the Jerusalem Jewish community—than that she is a woman. In the parenthetical comment, "(Jews do not share things in common with Samaritans)," for example, the Johannine narrator completely ignores how surprising it was that Jesus should speak to a woman, an indication that the Johannine faith community took the equal dignity of women for granted.

The point of this narrative from John's Gospel is to illustrate that Jesus offers the gift of salvation to all. The gospel's narrator could easily have told a story about an encounter between Jesus and another man, but he chose instead a story about a woman, and not just any woman but a woman whose past is checkered at best. Yet Jesus shows no scorn for this woman; instead, he offers her the gift of "living water" and reveals to her who he is.

While the important theological point here is undoubtedly Jesus' revelation of himself as Messiah, a man-woman relational issue is present as well—one that men in general, and married men in particular, should take to heart. Jesus' act of self-revelation to a woman to whom he accords full human dignity is a model for Catholic men in their relationships with women. Had Jesus simply demanded that the woman give him a drink of water and left it at that, the interaction would have remained superficial, and it would not have been a conversation between equals. It would have been a man-woman interaction typical of the culture of first-century Palestine. Instead, when the woman is so bold as to demand an explanation from Jesus for his request, Jesus immediately responds with words of self-revelation.

Jesus is the prime model for Catholic men in their relationships with women. Instead of merely going along with the dominant cultural model for male-female interactions, Jesus begins to tell the woman who he is. This, indeed, is the key to healthy marriages and other male-female relationships that "work." Men who rely on outmoded models that place men in a superior position vis-à-vis women, or women who "play games" to manipulate men are trying to live in a world that no longer exists.

By his example, the Jesus of the gospels invites men to be open to the self-revelation of women, and to be equally open in revealing themselves to women, particularly their wives. His actions tell men not to base their inner sense of self and their inner strength on any need to feel superior to women because this would be a false foundation. Instead, Jesus invites men to anchor their self-confidence in a healthy adult spirituality, in a mature faith relationship with him. Having this kind of secure foundation, rooted in faith, a man need not mask personal insecurity by trying to cultivate a macho attitude toward his wife or other women.

In particular, married Catholic men would do well to ignore the sectarian Christian conviction that God wants husbands to exercise "headship" over their wives. Fundamentalist Christians, for example, give a narrow, face-value interpretation to the following words from the Letter to the Ephesians:

> Wives, be subject to your husbands as you are to the Lord. For the husband is the head of the wife just as Christ is the head of the church, the body of which he is the Savior. Just as the church is subject to Christ, so also wives ought to be, in everything, to their husbands (5:22–24).

A fundamentalist reading of such words overlooks the cultural context in which they were written. Not only that, but a fundamentalist reading conveniently edits out the sentence that comes immediately before the words quoted above: "Be subject to one another out of reverence for Christ" (5:21). A fundamentalist perspective also tends to disregard the words that follow those quoted above: "Husbands, love your wives, just as Christ loved the church and gave himself up for her..." (5:25).

Even more important, fundamentalists overlook other radical scriptural insights that have an impact on relationships between men and women, such as these words from Paul's Letter to the Galatians:

> But now that faith has come...in Christ Jesus you are all children of God through faith. As many of you as were baptized into Christ have clothed yourselves with Christ. There is no longer Jew or Greek, there is no longer slave or free, there is no longer male and female; for all of you are one in Christ Jesus (3:25–28).

Scripture provides no justification for Catholic men and women to relate to one another on any but an equal basis: it's as simple as that. In marriage, husband and wife are equal partners, each bearing an equal responsibility to fashion a marriage that is satisfactory to both. Relationships in the workplace, including professional relationships between men and women in the Church, also rest on a basis of equality, mutual dignity, and mutual respect.

Returning to the explicit example of Jesus: in the Gospel of Mark, Jesus publicly disregards the cultural standards and religious legalisms of his own time in order to relate to a woman on a basis of human dignity:

> Now there was a woman who had been suffering from hemorrhages for twelve years. She had endured much under many physicians, and had spent all that she had; and she was no better, but rather grew worse. She had heard about Jesus, and came up behind him in the crowd and touched his cloak, for she said, "If I but touch his clothes, I will be made well." Immediately her hemorrhage stopped; and she felt in her body that she was healed of her disease. Immediately aware that power had gone forth from him, Jesus turned about in the crowd and said, "Who touched my clothes?" And his disciples said to him, "You see the crowd pressing in on you; how can you say, 'Who touched me?'" He looked all around to see who

had done it. But the woman, knowing what had happened to her, came in fear and trembling, fell down before him, and told him the whole truth. He said to her, "Daughter, your faith has made you well; go in peace, and be healed of your disease" (5:25–34).

Jesus allows himself to be touched by the woman with a menstrual disorder even though this makes him ritually unclean. He completely disregards this religious principle, however, in order to relate to the woman as a human being.

In Luke's Gospel, Jesus disregards sabbath regulations in order to cure "a woman with a spirit that had crippled her for eighteen years" (13:10–17).

Truth to tell, in the gospels Jesus heals an exceptionally large number of women. In Mark's Gospel, for example, Jesus heals [Simon] Peter's mother-in-law (1:29–31), Jairus' daughter (5:21–43), and the daughter of the Syrophoenician woman (7:24–30). Also in Mark, Jesus holds up as an example the "poor widow" who puts in the temple treasury "two small copper coins, which are worth a penny" (12:41–44). In both Mark (14:3–8) and John (12:1–8), Jesus defends Mary of Bethany for anointing his head and feet with oil.

In Luke, among the women Jesus heals is Mary Magdalene (8:2). Also in Luke, Jesus welcomes women among his disciples and accepts their help:

> Soon afterwards he went on through cities and villages, proclaiming and bringing the good news of the kingdom of God. The twelve were with him, as well as some women who had been cured of evil spirits and infirmities: Mary, called Magdalene, from whom seven demons had gone out, and Joanna, the wife of Herod's steward Chuza, and

Susanna, and many others, who provided for them out of their resources (8:1–3).

Notice that it is women who have been touched by Jesus, women who have experienced, firsthand, his healing power and his message of salvation, who stay with him as he travels "through cities and villages, proclaiming and bringing the good news of the kingdom of God." Luke offers such women as an example of how everyone should respond to Jesus.

Also in Luke, Jesus visits two sisters, Martha and Mary, and makes it clear that he wants *both* to listen to him: "Martha, Martha, you are worried and distracted by many things; there is need of only one thing. Mary has chosen the better part, which will not be taken away from her" (10:41–42).

When Jesus teaches about marriage in the gospels, his words are directed to men living in a culture that relegated women to the status of property. He also declares in no uncertain terms that adultery is unacceptable under any conditions, and his words are directed at men and women equally: "He said to them, 'Whoever divorces his wife and marries another commits adultery against her; and if she divorces her husband and marries another, she commits adultery'" (Mark 10:11–12). Catholic men will have nothing to do with any form of sexual activity outside of marriage. The dignity a Catholic man accords his wife, himself, and the holiness of their marriage allows for no extramarital sex.

The spirit of this teaching also applies to the single Catholic man, whose respect for himself and for his possible future spouse will not allow him to be sexually active before marriage. Cohabitation is not marriage, and only in superficial ways does it resemble marriage. Indeed, the higher divorce statistics among couples who have "lived together" prior to marriage merely confirm Jesus' concern for the dignity of women. As Laura Schlessinger, Ph.D., notes, "For women cohabitation is an audition, for men it is a convenience."[2] In the spirit of Jesus' teaching against adultery, Catholic men will be "old-fashioned" enough to save sex for marriage.[3]

Catholic men also need to take seriously that in all four gospels women are first to witness the empty tomb and carry the message to the male disciples. In John, for example, the risen Lord appears first to a woman, who then brings the good news of the Resurrection to the other disciples: "Mary Magdalene went and announced to the disciples, 'I have seen the Lord...'" (20:18).

Without question, men and women have equal dignity, in society, in marriage, and in the Church. Does this mean that women should be eligible for ordination as permanent deacons and priests? Liberal Catholics say yes, conservative Catholics say no, and it is possible that both camps are wrong for the present historical moment. The issue of women's ordination is far more complex than either side seems to think. For the foreseeable future, at least, the best response to this question may be "Who knows?" This is not an easy position to live with, but for now it may be the one closest to the truth and best for the Church as a whole.

Women's ordination is not the only gender-related issue fermenting in our Church. As we've discussed in previous chapters, other issues with major impact on parish life include the question of inclusive language in the liturgy and in Bible translations, and the predominance of women's influence in parish activities. Once again, men who would be Catholic in ways that are fair to all concerned do well to pay attention to the words and actions of the man Jesus in the gospels. Since Jesus' actions place men and women on a level playing field, does this mean that the Church should allow no role differences based on gender? The future will tell. What it does say to Catholic men, for one thing, is that they should not leave women to shoulder the preponderance of work in parishes. Men who "leave religion to women" fail to accept responsibility for using their own spiritual gifts to the fullest. Not only that, but a healthy parish needs to have both male and female perspectives in equal measure to balance and complement each other. Those men who "leave religion to women," and who fail to nourish their own masculine spirituality, have no right to complain if their parishes are not as "male friendly" as they are "female friendly."

Attitudes that maintain an imbalance between men and women active in the Church go back many generations, of course. In order for men to increase their active numbers, men who are active need to reach out to men who are not active. Once again, the man Jesus offers guidance. It may be no accident that as far as we can tell in his story of the Good Samaritan in the Gospel of Luke, all the characters are men. Read with this fact in mind:

"A man was going down from Jerusalem to Jericho, and fell into the hands of robbers, who stripped him, beat him, and went away, leaving him half dead. Now by chance a priest was going down that road; and when he saw him, he passed by on the other side. So likewise a Levite, when he came to the place and saw him, passed by on the other side. But a Samaritan while traveling came near him; and when he saw him, he was moved with pity. He went to him and bandaged his wounds, having poured oil and wine on them. Then he put him on his own animal, brought him to an inn, and took care of him. The next day he took out two denarii, gave them to the innkeeper, and said, 'Take care of him; and when I come back, I will repay you whatever more you spend.' Which of these three, do you think, was a neighbor to the man who fell into the hands of the robbers?" (10:30–36).

The typical interpretation of this story of Jesus overlooks the masculine character of the story, and in many situations this is perfectly understandable and acceptable. For our purposes, however, we highlight this fact: The main characters are both men, the man "going down from Jerusalem to Jericho," and the Samaritan himself. The priest and the Levite, also, are both men.

One question this story poses for Catholic men is this: Who am I in this story? An honest response would need to be "I am all the characters in this story." At one time or another, I am one of the robbers who takes advantage of someone else's defenselessness. I am the man taken advantage of by others. I am the priest and the Levite, neglecting to help. And I am the Samaritan, taking the trouble to care. Ideally, of course, Catholic men should think of themselves in the role of the Samaritan—in the context of our discussion, particularly when it comes to other men. Just as the Samaritan goes to the trouble and expense to help a man to whom violence has been done, so Catholic men would do well to go to some trouble and expense to help other men and draw them more into the life of the Church.

In our culture, men frequently are under tremendous pressure to conform to images of masculinity that deprive them of their own deepest center. Macho masculine images do this, but so do images of the male as computer whiz, the male as business honcho, and the male as sensitive guy. None of these images does a Catholic man justice at his deepest center, none nourishes his ontological union with the Divine Mystery. Only attention to the man Jesus and active participation in the living tradition of Catholicism can do this for a Catholic man, and then he needs a Church in which men are taken seriously, and parishes in which men are welcome on an equal basis with women.

Coming full circle, a Catholic man will find as he lives in relationships with women, and works alongside women, that his greatest strength and deepest vitality comes when he welcomes into his heart the man Jesus, as he finds him in the gospels. He discovers that in the man Jesus, he finds his deepest and truest self.

A Catholic man joins hands with the women in his life, turns the pages of the gospels, reads and listens closely, and the words are words of life. He listens and listens, and he realizes that the two words the risen man Jesus speaks to the man Peter in the fourth gospel are spoken to him, as well, always. A Catholic man listens and knows that in these two words are all he needs to know about being a man and being a Catholic. The words of the risen man Jesus thunder down through the centuries, and they are these: "Follow me" (John 21:19).

When all is said and done, this is what it means to be a Catholic man, to follow the risen man Jesus. These are the words that are the key to life now, and eternal life, for a Catholic man. This is the challenge, and this is the glory for a man who is Catholic—to follow him. It will always be so, world without end. Amen.

Afterword

A Catholic Man's Devotion to Mary

IN MONASTERIES of the Benedictine tradition each day concludes with the monastic office, or prayer, known in Latin as *compline*. This traditional night prayer includes chanting psalms, songs, and other prayers, but it also always includes the singing of what amounts to a good-night prayer to the Blessed Virgin Mary. Quite often this hymn is the traditional Catholic hymn to Mary called, in Latin, the *Salve Regina*. In English translation, the monks sing, "Hail, holy Queen, Mother of Mercy: Hail, our life, our sweetness, and our hope: To you do we cry, poor banished children of Eve....O clement, O loving, O sweet virgin Mary."

Many observers have, over the years, remarked that this monastic practice at the end of the day echoes the scene of a boy bidding a loving good night to his mother, and not without reason. Men need a feminine presence in their spirituality. The contemporary suggestion that men may, even should, satisfy this need by using feminine metaphors for God may work for some men, and if so that is fine. Both men and women are created in the image of God; therefore, both masculine and feminine metaphors may be used to image God. Whether this approach will catch on remains to be seen. Beginning in its early decades, however, Christianity met the masculine need for a feminine component in spirituality by encouraging devotion to the Blessed Virgin Mary.

Christianity is and always has been a monotheistic father religion. But Christianity cultivated a devotion to Mary, the mother of Jesus, and Roman Catholicism, as well as the Orthodox Churches and, to a lesser degree, the churches of the Anglican communion, maintains this devotion down to the present day. Marian devotion contributes a balancing feminine dimension to the faith of Catholics in the midst of a religion that follows the example of Jesus, who always called God his *Abba,* or "loving Papa."

Catholic men follow Jesus. They turn to him as "true God and true man," and they are well advised to focus on his masculinity as they read and meditate upon the gospels and the other New Testament documents. In this way, Catholic men can learn to make their faith the foundation of their life in a culture that offers phony models of masculinity. They can learn to live a masculine faith in the footsteps of the man Jesus and in communion with the risen Christ.

The *Catechism of the Catholic Church,* quoting Saint Augustine and Pope Paul VI, calls Mary "'clearly the mother of the members of Christ'

> ...since she has by her charity joined in bringing about the birth of believers in the Church, who are members of its head. 'Mary, Mother of Christ, Mother of the Church'" (963).

Catholic men will find their faith enriched by praying the rosary in particular. Men often find this centuries-old form of Marian devotion beneficial because it is both simple and profound. David Burton Bryan, Ph.D., calls the rosary "clearly the world's single most popular form of meditation."[1] Men who associate nonmasculine images with the rosary would do well to recall that, according to legend, the Blessed Virgin Mary gave the rosary to a man, Saint Dominic, and the most influential proponent of the rosary in the twentieth century was a man, Father Patrick Peyton, C.S.C.

As a devotional prayer to Mary, the rosary suits a masculine spirituality because it brings a man into intimacy with the mother of Jesus, and this relationship serves as a feminine balance to his love for the God whom Jesus teaches him to call *Abba*, "Father." Devotion to Mary, in general, can also be helpful to a man because it conditions his attitudes toward and relationships with women. In this regard, it is important for men to stay close to the Mary of the Gospels of Matthew and Luke, a young woman who is both strong in faith, bold in her dignity, and willing to trust completely in God's will for her.[2]

A masculine approach to being Catholic is rooted in ongoing intimacy with the Jesus of the gospels and with the risen Christ alive and active here and now. Along the way, however, men would do well to take personally the words of Jesus in John's Gospel as, from the cross, he gives his mother, Mary, to the beloved disciple. Jesus says to him, and by extension to men who follow him today, "Here is your mother" (19:27). A man does well to take Jesus' mother as his mother, too. Thus there will be a warm, constant place in a man's spirituality for companionship with Mary as he dedicates himself daily to her son who is the risen Christ.

Notes

Notes to Preface

1. *Declaration on the Relationship of the Church to Non-Christian Religions,* no. 2.
2. G. K. Chesterton, *The Well and the Shallows* (London, 1935) 71–72.
3. Mitch Finley, *The Seeker's Guide to Being Catholic* (Chicago: Loyola Press, 1997).

Notes to Introduction

1. Among these are the following: *The Wild Man's Journey: Reflections on Male Spirituality* by Richard Rohr and Joseph Martos (Cincinnati: St. Anthony Messenger Press, 1992); *Wildmen, Warriors, and Kings: Masculine Spirituality and the Bible* by Patrick M. Arnold, S.J. (New York: Crossroad Publishing Co., 1991); *A Man and His God: Contemporary Male Spirituality* by Martin W. Pable, O.F.M.Cap. (Notre Dame, Indiana: Ave Maria Press, 1988); *Toward a Male Spirituality* by John Carmody (Mystic, Connecticut: Twenty-Third Publications, 1989); *He: Understanding Masculine Psychology* by Robert A. Johnson (King of Prussia, Pennsylvania: Religious Publishing Co., 1974).
2. Arnold, 185.

Notes to Chapter 1

1. Edward Collins Vacek, S.J., "The Eclipse of Love for God," *America* 174:8 (March 9, 1996). See also Edward Collins Vacek, S.J., *Love, Human and Divine: The Heart of Christian Ethics* (Washington, D.C.: Georgetown University Press, 1994).
2. From many of his public presentations.
3. Thomas Merton, *The Asian Journal of Thomas Merton*, ed. Naomi Burton, Brother Patrick Hart, and James Laughlin; consulting ed. Amiya Chakravarty (New York: New Directions, 1973).
4. Thomas Merton, *Thoughts in Solitude* (New York: Farrar, Straus and Giroux, 1956) 17.

Notes to Chapter 2

1. Abraham Joshua Heschel, *Between God and Man* (New York: Free Press, 1959, 1997) 35.
2. Our approach to the gospels in this book is not that of the Scripture scholar or exegete. We do take for granted the historical-critical methods of biblical interpretation, as well as criticism of such methods that would balance historical-critical interpretation with other methods meant to put us more in touch with the spiritual, pastoral, and ecclesial meanings of Scripture. We also adopt the perspective that philosopher Paul Ricoeur calls "second naiveté." We acknowledge that the authors of the gospels were editors and narrative theologians with specific theological perspectives. We acknowledge the historical processes that went into the development of the unique portrait of Jesus found in each gospel, but we put this knowledge in brackets, if you will. We do not revert to fundamentalist narrow-mindedness, but we set aside scientific interpretation of the gospels for the moment. We simply look at the Jesus of the gospels to see what he may teach a man today about being both a man and a disciple of Christ.

Notes to Chapter 3

1. Laura Schlessinger, Ph.D., *Ten Stupid Things Men Do to Mess Up Their Lives* (New York: HarperCollins, 1997) 38.
2. Ibid., 39.

3. See Andrew M. Greeley, *God in Popular Culture* (Chicago: Thomas More Press, 1988).
4. See John W. Miller, *Biblical Faith and Fathering: Why We Call God "Father"* (Mahwah, New Jersey: Paulist Press, 1989).

Notes to Chapter 4

1. See Patrick F. McManus, *The Night the Bear Ate Goombaw* (New York: Henry Holt, 1993) and *Into the Wilderness, Endlessly Grousing* (New York: Simon & Schuster, 1997).
2. James Lee Burke, *Heaven's Prisoners* (New York: Pocket Books, 1978) 27.
3. Tony Castle, comp., *The New Book of Christian Quotations* (New York: Crossroad Publishing Co., 1989) 86.

Notes to Chapter 5

1. Pope John Paul II, *The Pope Speaks to the American Church* (San Francisco: HarperSanFrancisco, 1992) 223.
2. Arlene Rossen Cardozo, *Jewish Family Celebrations* (New York: St. Martin's Press, 1982) xiii.
3. For more historical information, see *The HarperCollins Encyclopedia of Catholicism* (San Francisco: HarperSanFrancisco, 1995) 517.
4. See Karl Rahner, S.J., "Love for God and Human Beings" in *The Practice of Faith* (New York: Crossroad Publishing Co., 1983) 125.
5. There is some question today about whether Jesus' preference for calling God his *Abba* is merely a metaphor. If so, Christians may, for example, call God "Mother" more or less arbitrarily. If Jesus' preference for calling God his Father is more than a metaphor, however—if in some sense verbal inspiration kicks in here—then Christians are not free to give "Mother" equal status with "Father" when addressing God.
6. Clayton C. Barbeau, *The Father of the Family,* revised ed. (San Francisco: Ikon Books, 1990) 120.

Notes to Chapter 6

1. One recalls Flannery O'Connor's remark about "the clerical gift for bringing forth the sonorous familiar phrase of slowly deadening effect." See *The Presence of Grace and Other Book Reviews by Flannery O'Connor,* compiled by Leo J. Zuber, edited and with introduction by Carter W. Martin (Athens, Georgia: University of Georgia Press, 1983) 148.
2. Andrew M. Greeley, *The Bishop at Sea* (Berkely Books, 1997).
3. Joan Peters of Saint Cecilia Parish, Houston, Texas, interviewed by Charles Morris, "A Tale of Two Dioceses," *Commonweal* (June 6, 1997).
4. Avery Dulles, S.J., *Models of the Church* (New York: Doubleday, 1974).
5. Avery Dulles, S.J., *Models of the Church: Expanded Edition* (New York: Doubleday Image Books, 1987) 10.

Notes to Chapter 7

1. G. K. Chesterton, *Charles Dickens* (London, 1906) 62.
2. John W. Miller, *Biblical Faith and Fathering: Why We Call God "Father"* (Mahwah, New Jersey: Paulist Press, 1989) 112.

Notes to Chapter 8

1. Richard P. McBrien, *Catholicism,* revised ed. (HarperSanFrancisco, 1994) 898.
2. Laura Schlessinger, Ph.D., *Ten Stupid Things Women Do to Mess Up Their Lives* (Villard Books, 1994) 102.
3. See also Michael J. McManus, *Marriage Savers* (Zondervan Publishing House, 1993), especially the section titled "Cohabitation Does Not Work," 91–93.

Notes to Afterword

1. David Burton Bryan, Ph.D., *A Western Way of Meditation: The Rosary Revisited* (Chicago: Loyola Press, 1991) xi.
2. See my book *Surprising Mary: Meditations and Prayers on the Mother of Jesus* (Williston Park, New York: Resurrection Press, 1997).

www.ingramcontent.com/pod-product-compliance
Lightning Source LLC
Chambersburg PA
CBHW050829160426
43192CB00010B/1959